Stop Should-*ing*

Start Wanting

Judith Quin

This edition is published by
That Guy's House in 2018

© Copyright 2018, Judith Quin
All rights reserved.

No part of this publication may be reproduced, stored, in a retrieval system, or transmitted, in any form or by any means without permission of the publisher.

www.ThatGuysHouse.com

hey,

Welcome to this wonderful book brought to you by That Guy's House Publishing.

At That Guy's House we believe in real and raw wellness books that inspire the reader from a place of authenticity and honesty.

This book has been carefully crafted by both the author and publisher with the intention that it will bring you a glimmer of hope, a rush of inspiration and sensation of inner peace.

It is our hope that you thoroughly enjoy this book and pass it onto friends who may also be in need of a glimpse into their own magnificence.

Have a wonderful day.

Love,

Sean Patrick

That Guy.

I'd like to dedicate this book to Bruce and Barbara Buchan.

Bruce was my first vocal confidence client and that wouldn't have happened if, during a massage, Barbara hadn't said:

"Judith, you're an actress, and you do that 'stuff' with sound.

Bruce hates speaking in public and has to deliver a speech to 80 solicitors in a couple of weeks, do you know anyone who could help him?"

Without Bruce's success, other massage clients wouldn't have found out what I was doing, it wouldn't have been suggested by one of them that I look at training to be a coach – this book wouldn't be here!

Bruce – you are hugely missed.

Barbara – Without your question where would I be?

THANK YOU.

With love

A bit about the author

Judith is a vocal confidence specialist, coach, holistic healer, and actress. Some people might say she 'should' say "actor"~ she doesn't really care.

She has spent her life finding herself speaking up for other people, maybe sometimes when they didn't want her to! Now she spends her life empowering people to find their own voice, so they can speak with confidence for themselves.

Based in London, and always eager to travel, she works both with individuals and in the corporate world. The core of her work focuses on reconnecting you to who you really are, to what is important to you, and using the power of voice vibration to release the thoughts and feelings that have been holding you back.

That done, connected to your true, whole, self, you can start to find your true, whole voice so when you speak, you do so with more confidence and with less fear of judgment by others.

Running group workshops and seminars, talking at events as an international public speaker, or working privately with individuals, Judith gets a buzz from helping people find, free, and use their confident voice. Often the first step to this is coming back to yourself, reminding yourself of what is important to *you*, and thereby knowing what it is you *want* to communicate.

If you are looking for the confidence to express yourself, if you're a leader who has had a life or business event happen that has shaken you, if you are starting out, or starting again, and not sure where you stand, or what you're doing – Judith believes it's all connected to whether you are listening to your inner voice telling you what YOU *really* want.

Judith also works with the voice through sonic meditation and sound healing, in which there is no 'right' way to sound; no 'shoulds'. This helps people accept their voice, reconnect their voice to their body, and escape the mental, physical and emotional noise around expressing themselves.

At the time of writing, Judith is in the process of creating a combined sound healing and vocal confidence retreat.

Occasionally she gets paid to act!

Foreword

Judith Quin combines her years of experience and skills to create powerful transformations for people in their lives. It is part of the reason why I invited her to join the Association of Transformational Leaders of Europe.

With her sensitivity, humour and elegance, she is able to give you transformational insights and create exercises for you to help you find the path that is right for you.

Judith is a powerful international "Public Speaking coach". She helps you to discover your own power by finding your confident, powerful, voice.

By finding out where your blocks are, she then establishes how you can find and "free your voice" in order to express that.

In this book, Judith walks you through the start of that transformational journey by providing a variety of exercises. By working through some of your challenges, Judith helps you to listen to your inner voice and supports you in reconnecting to what is really important to you.

Once you know what it is you want, you can start creating it. But if you're living a life that is restricted by feeling like you 'should', then what you create won't be in alignment with your true self and your voice will be restricted.

This book is about finding and listening to your own voice, an introduction to simple coaching methods, and making positive choices; it is an essential step to living the life that you WANT.

I highly recommend that you start working with the powerful and transformational tools and exercises Judith Quin provides for you. It is life changing.

Marie Diamond

Global Transformational Teacher, Speaker, Best Selling International Author, Master Teacher and Star in The Secret and President of the Association of Transformational Leaders for Europe.

www.MarieDiamond.com

What people are saying about "Stop 'Should-ing'. Start Wanting."

"It's really brilliant, super insightful, and full of really easy to follow practical steps and great questions. It's a really great balance of education with practical tools and getting to know you, too."
Sophie French (Copywriter)

"I think the real break-through for me is that it's brought to the forefront that I spend too much time looking back and thinking 'oh if only this or that.' I think I'm going to make 'Stop wanting. Start creating' my new mantra!"
Dhivya O'Connor (COO Children With Cancer)

"I love this. It's a helpful tool and a lovely read."
Abi McLaughlin (actress)

"I Really liked it!! There was a great tone throughout, and the exercises were helpful, particularly the numbering. I did this as I went and when you categorised them it became quite clear to me my actual wants."
James Cole

"I felt I "should" read it because it was from you and secondly I was not keen as "no time" and I read too slow. Also I did not want to let anyone down!!. I started to read and to my surprise I wanted to continue until I finished!"
Dee Graham

"The exercises were clear and moved you along on building from one point to the next."

Lesley Coburn (Reflexologist, NLP)

"I did enjoy doing the exercises and loved reading your personal input. Even though I have done many similar exercises the way you set out your exercises made them feel fresh. I would recommend/buy it for someone who I thought needed a little nudge."

(Roberta Ardern)

I was supposed to be putting reading your book on the 'back burner', to enable me to progress with my own book, against a tight deadline, but found myself at Exercise 1 before I knew it!

(Roger Cheetham)

Amazon 5* Reviews

Thank you for a timely reminder.

The book is well written and easy to read, with the exercises providing useful action steps to really make positive changes. Words have power and "should" is a word I will be "wanting" to erase from my vocabulary, and, in particular, from my self-talk! Thank you Judith, I look forward to your next book.

(JC Groom)

A timely and much needed advice on how to start listening to your own needs, engage intuition and own your choices. With personal stories many of us can relate to, this book makes an easy and entertaining reading, and gives simple tools to practice in everyday life. Got it yesterday and couldn't stop reading, highly recommend to all who are determined to make their life happier!

(Anastasia Pavlova)

What a fantastic read!! Well worth some time to read this and focus on your self-development and can't think of a better book to kick start that journey.

(Anon)

Absolutely fantastic, I can't highly recommend it enough

(Kezia Luckett)

Contents Page

Introduction to the book: xv

Take it easy xix

How does 'should' and 'want' relate to finding my voice?"... xx

Part 1 "Why Should I?" 1

   My Light-bulb Moment 2

   I didn't WANT to. 3

   Free from 'Should' 7

   Getting Going.. 10

   Exercise 1... 11

   The next step....................................... 19

   Making Choices ~ Liberation from 'should'.. 21

   The Yes's (8-10's)................................... 26

   The Maybe's (4-7) 27

   The No's (1-3).. 31

   Consequences & Choices 34

   "But I HAVE to" 41

   Exercise 2... 43

   The reversie 'Should'.............................. 49

   Exercise 3... 52

   Are any of your shouldn'ts obvious wants? . 55

Part 2 'Shoulding' Your Life 63
    Your Life-Shoulds. 65
    The Wake-up Call. 72
    Life-Shoulds 73
    Exercise 4 76
    Whose Shoulds Be These? 79
    Changing your perspective 90
    Changing the Energy 92
    Exercises Review 94

Part 3 "What's Stopping You?" 97
    What's In Your Way: The Blocks 99
    Reasons or Excuses? 101
    The "Battle of The 'But's" 104
    The Voices of Doom 111
    Exercise 5 115
    Beware Blame! 117
    Perspective & Focus 123
    Staying Safe or Future Focus? 131
    Moving Forward 140

Message from the Author 146

About the Illustrator: 148

Acknowledgments: 149

Introduction to the book:

"What research have you done, Judith?"

"Tried to decide on the book size, how frequent the illustrations should be, what the word count might be and a couple of possible publishers."

"You should probably do some research."

"No I shouldn't. Or I'll never write it!"

This was a conversation that happened purely in my head! Thankfully I ignored my 'should' thoughts and got writing!

So, if you have read, or written, something similar about this topic, please trust that I have not ripped anyone off ... We just believe the same things, and live by the same belief; that 'To should' isn't very useful.

Great! In my book, (no pun intended!) the more people we can share that with, the better.

The ideas in this book have been inspired by my life, and compounded that they were a good way to live when I trained as a coach with The Coaching Academy.

In fact, I'd lived for seventeen years with "don't should" as a concept which I didn't hear from anyone else, until I was at a two-day coaching discovery course where suddenly I heard other people talking about 'should-ing' the way that I did!

Yet more proof that there is nothing unique or new in this world, but the way we experience things is always unique to us.

I hope you enjoy the experience of this book and its exercises, they have been created to help you:

Find Your Voice

Discover what it is YOU *want*

Feel more in control of your life.

Feeling obliged, or like you ***should*** do something, often brings with it a sense of resentment, or heaviness.

Whether it's the job you go to, the life you are living, or the pile of washing and ironing that needs doing; if on some level you don't ***want*** to, satisfaction levels will be low.

Do you often find yourself doing, or going to, things that you don't really want to?

Do you feel obliged?

Are you living a life full of doing things for other people, or because they are expected of you, or something you felt you ought to do, or say, but which doesn't fit with your values, or with where you want to be in the world?

If you find yourself regularly thinking or saying things like:

"I *should* …"

"I *have* to..."

"I really *ought* to ..."

Then this book is for you. To help you find *your* voice, knowing what it is *you* want, and how *you* want to live.

This is an introductory book, intended to assist you in listening to your inner voice, adjusting your mindset when it comes to making choices and living your life with less obligation and more desire.

It is an experiential book, with exercises for you to complete and techniques to use, which help you look at your 'shoulds'. The aim is to find ways to either; turn that sense of duty in to desire, or, with big relief, bin them from your life altogether!

Within the book I share a couple of personal experiences and stories of my own past 'shoulds', where they came from, and their effects. They are mostly to do with my desire to be an actor.

I share these to highlight how easy it is for us to be distracted from the path we really want to be on. Hopefully these stories will help you look at your own 'shoulding' so you can start to explore where your "should" thoughts, feelings, and beliefs come from.

There are many reasons why we do, or don't do, things, why we believe we should be doing something a certain way. Most of the time we don't even know that we are living our 'shoulds' in that way!

You can, of course, read the book without doing the exercises ~ a couple of my first-draft readers did that and then said they'd go back to them later ~ but I promise the book will have more effect if you do.

Of course, though, if you don't "want" to – that's your choice.

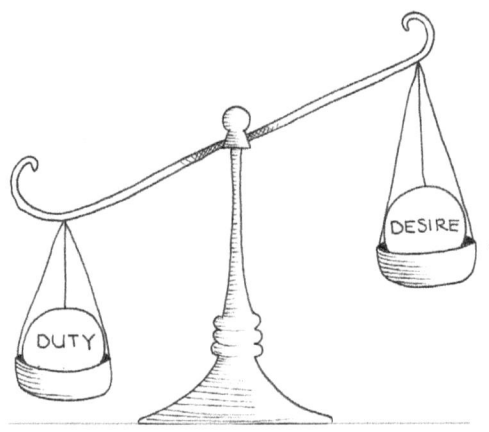

Take it easy

This book is not intended as therapy, or as a healing tool, however, the nature of coaching means that in the book I do encourage you to challenge yourself, to look at the way you approach some elements of your life.

When we look at making choices and changing the way we think, it brings up the patterns we use which come from our past. This may bring up elements from your life that might be mentally or emotionally challenging.

If you feel that might be a possibility for you, or if you have experienced trauma in your past, I encourage you to be aware of this when you do the exercises. If the exercises do bring up things from your life that are challenging for you, I encourage you to work with something lighter and maybe find a professional who can help.

Alternatively, you can always skip an exercise if it's bringing up things that you are uncomfortable with. This book is about doing what is right for YOU and you can start by choosing how to make the book itself work best for you.

"You're a vocal confidence specialist…. How does 'should' and 'want' relate to finding my voice?"

Finding your voice isn't all about speaking in public, sharing a thought, feeling, or opinion with a friend or family member, or speaking up in a work meeting, can be just as challenging. I am a firm believer that *all* speaking is public speaking, but that's different topic for another day!

We all have two voices; our social voice and our expressive voice.

We may well adapt, or censor, these voices depending on the situation we find ourselves in, and that is a perfectly normal way of adjusting, or fitting in, to the world around us.

How you are at home is often different to how you are at work, or with old friends, for example, and that is fine. Often we adapt, adjust, or censor, what we want to say to keep a balanced atmosphere, or if something doesn't feel appropriate at that time.

However, if you feel you are always adjusting for others, or if what you are saying doesn't match with what you believe, what you value at your core, there is a problem; a disconnect.

Your social voice is your inner voice; that which you think and feel, the things you believe in and stand for. (This voice can develop and change with age, experience and awareness).

Your expressive voice is how you share your social voice - in other words, what you say. (Your confidence in using this voice can vary and depend on the situation you are in, who you're with, or past experiences).

That expression may take several forms:

Vocally: through speaking.

Manually: through the written word.

Physically: through the actions you take, or don't take, (like protesting for example – it's a way of expressing what you feel strongly about).

Your expressive voice is how you put your social voice out to the world, I am expressing my social (or inner) voice through this, my first book. If I'm honest, the thought of putting this book out there to the world felt vulnerable, much more so than standing on a stage and speaking.

If I'm REALLY honest – when this was first released on Kindle, I spent the whole first day terrified that a) it wouldn't sell to anyone but good friends and family and b) massive imposter syndrome kicked in with thoughts of not being good enough. But I have to practice what I preach, and it's been three years since I had the initial idea …. So it was time to take action! (Thankfully the response has been fabulous – and not just from my mum and dad!)

When you have a lot of 'should' in your life you may very well find you are regularly suppressing your true voice, what you really believe, think, or feel;

often to placate, please, or avoid the perceived judgment of, others. Sometimes this suppression may be because it is not appropriate, or because you don't want to hurt someone's feelings, or be rude, or you don't have the energy to contradict someone, and so you make a choice to ignore or go along with what someone else has said.

This is perfectly normal, and in some situations a great idea.

Sometimes, however, people end up suppressing their inner, social, voice so regularly that it becomes habit, they forget how to express themselves. They are *living* their (or other people's) 'shoulds'. Often this is because the habit of compromise has become a way of life. This may have started out with good reason, to get the best results for all people in a family, social, or work situation, for example. However, that can end up with you living a life you feel disconnected with, a life of 'should'; rather than knowing and following what it is YOU want to say or do.

When you stop living your 'shoulds', and start making choices which follow your highest-purpose desires, when you know what it is that YOU *really* want, it's much easier to express yourself, and speak with, or from, your heart.

So that is how 'shoulds' and 'wants' are connected to vocal confidence.

First, know your inner self and connect it with your higher-purpose, then learn how to express yourself.

This book is not just for those who find speaking up challenging – I've rarely had a problem expressing myself vocally – however, I have had my fair share of 'should' thoughts in my life…

Part 1
"Why Should I?"

"Because I said so."

My Light-bulb Moment

The first time I freed myself from "should" was in September 1997, I was in Chicago, sitting by the shore of Lake Michigan.

I'd been travelling on my own for just under three months, across Canada from east to west, then down in to the States, and was heading back, west to east. I'd been to some amazing places and seen and done some wonderful things and I found myself thinking "I really should go to the contemporary art museum …"

But in the previous three months I think I'd already been to more museums and art galleries than in the whole of the nearly 24 years of my life, it was a beautiful day and I was tired and on my own, I had no-one else to please …. oh …. and it wasn't free entry that day[1].

So, there I was, sitting by the lake thinking, "I really should go …"

Then I had a ground-breaking realisation …

---

[1] Backpackers are tight with money, especially when you've not long been on the road, have gone the costlier route ~ America ~ rather than India/Nepal/Far East-Asia, and haven't fully realised the point that you may never be back!

I didn't WANT to.

I had no-one and nothing to be beholden to, so why should I feel like I *should*?

Because the 'Lonely Planet' or 'Rough Guide' said so? (Remember this was 1997 - a time before the internet revolution, before Trip Advisor or 'e-books' - a time when all backpackers carried multiple hard copies of these vast tomes with them)!

Because others would expect me to have been?

Because I was <u>there</u>?

Because I'd tried to go the day before and got there 15 minutes before closing and felt like I'd missed out on something?

So that, when I bumped in to other travellers, I could say; "Yes, yes … I went there … Yes, wasn't it … whatever"?

Yes.

All those things were making me feel like I *should*. I should 'do my duty' and see another Monet or something. But the point was:

I DIDN'T *WANT* TO.

Then I started thinking about the other things I had done in life because I 'should', and the things I didn't do because I felt I 'Shouldn't' (like not skipping one afternoon of 6th Form college with my friends to go and meet Skid Row because you 'shouldn't' bunk off school[2])

I realised that SHOULD (and shouldn't) come with a whole heap of other people's conditioning and expectations *and often a sense of not wanting to.*

I no longer wanted to live like that. At the very least not right then, not while I was backpacking around the world on my own, with no-one else to be beholden, please, or live up to.

So, I thought about the museum and I didn't want to go.

So, I didn't!

When I started thinking about writing this book I couldn't remember exactly where or when the moment happened. I knew it was quite early on in my 2¼ year trip.

What I could remember clearly was the delight and freedom of realising that I had expunged a

---

[2] It was 1991 Skid Row were a long-haired rock band fronted by the ridiculously beautiful lead singer, Sebastian Bach. It wouldn't have been the end of the world if I had gone with my friends, but I didn't go because I didn't want to let my mum down if she found out I'd skipped college, and so I missed out on an experience they had, one which I really wanted.
This helped instigate another of my core live-by beliefs: "You only regret the things that you really want to do in life, but don't."

word from my vocabulary, I had changed a concept in my life ...

I would no longer "Should"

It has turned out to be one of the moments that has helped shape my life, my mindset, and the way I live.

I went back through my travel journals to see if I could find whether this 'Eureka' moment was big enough at the time for me to acknowledge. I hunted and read to see if I'd written it down, if I'd marked the moment – it turns out I didn't. However, when I read what I'd written, sat by Lake Michigan having decided to not go to the museum, I knew it was then, the same feeling of changing my plans hit me.

Who wouldn't change plans? It was a hot, sunny, day and instead of spending it inside, before another 27 hours on a Greyhound bus, I wanted to walk around the vast, sea-like, lake shore.

Free from 'Should'

From my photo album – yes – that's right! An actual hard copy album, filled with images taken on a camera that had film in it – I didn't see this photo until two years after I took it, because I sent my rolls of film home to be developed at the shop I used to work in – did I mention backpackers are pretty tight with money?!

I'm sure some of you are reading this thinking:

"What's this got to do with me?"

and/or

"That's all very well, a 23year old backpacker on their own is free to not 'should', but I've got things in my life that I *have* to do that I *really* should".

("Have to" "Need to" and "Ought" are also often big 'should's but we'll come to that later, because we don't *have* to do anything – there is always a choice, usually a consequence, but always a choice).

What it has to do with you, is that we all have a few 'shoulds' that would feel better becoming something we 'want' to do, or would feel amazing to let go of.

So let's start to look at yours.

Getting Going

So, you've got things in your life that you feel obliged by? Things you feel like you *have* to do, that you *really* should. They feel a bit heavy, or annoying, maybe they make you sigh at the thought of them. That's OK. You can make a choice and either turn them in to a want, or ditch them from your life altogether!

As mentioned at the start of the book, your "shoulds" for these exercises can be as big or as trivial as you like, they can be long-term, immediate, or a mix of both.

If you are prone to over thinking, emotional anxiety, or the like, then use a 'should' that's not too pressing, like 'I should do the ironing'.

(Old-fashioned pun not intended .. but I like it now it's there!)

Exercise 1.

On the next page, write down a list of five things you feel like you really SHOULD either: be, be doing, or have in your life right now.

For example, mine might read:

"I should…"

1) Lose 7lbs

2) Write this book

3) Finish writing my play

4) Stop occasionally sleeping with my ex-boyfriend

5) Cover up (I wrote the first draft in the sun on holiday – I'm half Irish and despite factor 30 I was about to burn)!

"I should …."

1) ………………………………………………………

2) ………………………………………………………

3) ………………………………………………………

4) ………………………………………………………

5) ………………………………………………………

Now feel free to tear out this page and take it with you as we move on.

If you have real issues with tearing pages out of, or writing in, books "I shouldn't – it's a book!!!" then use a pencil so you can do it again at a later date, or take a separate piece of paper and write your list on that.

I ask you to write it on paper rather than a phone or tablet, as the action of physically writing solidifies your thought process.

Don't 'Should'

"Want"

You now have your first list of shoulds.

It might include the big things in life like; 'be married by now', 'get a new job', 'have children', or more every-day things like; 'do the ironing' or 'wash the car', or in relation to speaking; 'ask for what I need', 'share my ideas in team meetings', 'deliver that presentation', 'create that workshop', or 'do that wedding speech'.

It really doesn't matter what your 'shoulds' are; it's whatever **you** feel you **'should'** *be* in your life, be *doing* in your life, or *have* in your life, at this moment. (You can do this exercise as often as you like, so for now just use what came to mind first).

Look at your list and think about whether you **want** to do them and write "yes" or "no" next to your 'should'.

It is important that you are honest with yourself here, make sure you're writing down whether or not YOU want those things on your list – be selfish.

This is key, as it's all about you.

This exercise is not about what is right for others, or what others' expectations of, or for, you are – this is YOUR feeling about that should.

It's just an exercise, and we're just starting, so go with this here; otherwise it won't work and it's only yourself you're lying to.

Don't panic if you want to say "No" even if affects other people, or you feel they may suffer if you follow it through – we will come to that later.

If you really can't make up your mind as to 'yes' or 'no' – there is always 'maybe'.

What do your shoulds look like now?

Mine looked like this:

Do I WANT to?

1) Lose 7lbs - Kind of

2) Write this book - Yes

3) Finish my play – At some point – it's been half written for 5 years

4) Stop occasionally sleeping with my ex-boyfriend - Not really

5) Cover up (to not burn) - No

What are you starting to think, feel, or notice about your 'shoulds'?

Are they easy for you to relate to, or hard to get your head around how to make it happen?

Do they make you feel inspired and excited, or a bit obliged and heavy?

Do some of them make you sigh? Do some of them make you smile?

Start sorting

The next step.

Now I want you to give each of your 'shoulds' a score out of ten as to how much you **want** to do, be, or have it in your life:

1 being "I really don't want (to do) it" and **10** being "Hell yeah – I want that".

Write that down after your yes or no thought.

Now you have somewhere to begin.

You probably have a mix of things you *want* to do, *don't want* to do and possibly, kind-of want, or know would be good for you … but don't really want enough to put in to action, yet not enough to let go of either.

There's one last step before we start looking at your shoulds in detail.

Look at the number you've assigned, but now with the below categories in mind:

1-3 – "NO I don't want to do/be/have that (even if I know it would be good for me, or others, – I just don't want it right now)"

4-7 – "Yes, I feel like I probably should, a part of me does want it but I'm not entirely convinced."

Or

"It might be good for me to do that, but I'm in some way comfortable with, or attached to, my current situation, and it's not that much of a 'thing' for me"

OR

"I'm not sure I really believe I can"

8-10 – "I WANT that, it might seem difficult or far away, it might be really simple and I've just not done it, but I KNOW I want it."

With the above in mind, if you now want to make any changes to your numbers, go ahead, change them, they're YOUR shoulds and your numbers.

Nothing is fixed in stone here, not even the 'shoulds' – you want to replace one of them with something else? Go ahead. Or you can always just do the exercise again later with a different list of shoulds!

How is your list looking? Mine would look now like this:

1) Lose 7lbs - Kind of - 5
2) Write this book – Yes - 10
3) Finish my play – At some point -it's been half written for 5 years - 6
4) Stop occasionally sleeping with my ex-boyfriend - Not really - 4
5) Cover up (so I don't burn)! – No – 2

So, you can see – I have one obvious want on my list, a bunch of 'kind ofs' and a really silly, childish, stroppy 'no'

But – they feel about right to me.

What do you think about yours? How do yours look, or feel, to you: on a 'want' level?

If they don't feel true – then adjust the yes, no, maybe, or number.

Making Choices ~ Liberation from 'should'.

Now that you have your list of 'shoulds' and you know how much you want, or don't want, them, how do you make a 'should' a 'want'?

How can you create something that you can look forward to doing, being, having, or completing in life?

You choose.

We all have to make choices in life, for all of our wants, don't wants, and undecided's, and be happy to live with the consequences of making those choices.

This is part of getting to know your inner, social, voice. Learning what you really want and how much you are willing to change, or back that up, with your actions.

There are the simple yes or no choices:

YES - where you decide you want it and put a plan in to action to be it, do it or have it.

NO – where you decide you don't want it and let it go.

Then there are the slightly more complicated 'undecided's where you might choose to live with it a bit longer and deal with it when you can't ignore it any more.

Annoyingly, there are also the 'No' feelings that are REALLY STRONG shoulds, or "HAVE TO". These are the ones that, as much as you might not want, or *really* don't want – you know that it is better for you, or for others, if you do. (Like my ex-boyfriend choice I knew it would definitely be better for me to make the choice to stop ... it took a while to actually make that choice and take that action though!)

For example, you know it might be detrimental to others, or to yourself, if you don't like making supper, doing the washing, or taking the kids to school ... But there *is* still a choice.

We can still transform these 'shoulds' into 'want' ... if we choose to.

Every choice has a consequence, including staying where you are and choosing to change nothing.

Sometimes the consequences are beneficial to our lives and to those around us, sometimes we think they'll be beneficial and they're not, sometimes we think they'll be challenging, or hurtful, to others but actually they liberate them, sometimes those consequences may well hurt or disrupt someone else's life, sometimes they'll inspire others to make a brilliant choice of their own.

We can't always see what the consequences of our actions might be, sometimes we think they'll be better or worse than they actually are, sometimes we're right.

All I know is that every situation provides us with a choice and we can choose to stay where we are, or move one step (or maybe a leap) in a specific, chosen, direction. If that proves detrimental, we can choose a new step, if it proves beneficial, take another.

"The one thing you can't take away from me is the way I choose to respond to what you do to me.

The last of one's freedoms is to choose one's attitude in any given circumstance."

Viktor E. Frankl (Death Camp Survivor) *Man's Search for Meaning*

The Yes's (8-10's)

The yes's can be relatively easy, because the drive is there, things might come up or get in our way, but if we really want to, we'll find a way to make it happen.

This book is a case in point – I really wanted to write this book, I was on holiday and writing the book is how much I wanted it; technically, on holiday, working!

However, I'm actually writing this sentence over a year later because things came up in life, my priorities shifted once I got home, I let myself believe I didn't have the time and other things became more pressing.

BUT, I got to the point when this book became a priority again and am now getting up at 6:15 every morning for a month (at least) specifically to write this book for an hour (at least).

I created the time I thought I didn't have, in order to focus on my want, to re-write and finish this book. Case in point, the month of 6:15 got the bulk started but I'm finishing this first draft on holiday, again!

So, how are you going to get your 8 – 10 wants done, or created?

Finish this book & get started!

The Maybe's (4-7)

The ambiguous 4 – 7 section can be pesky. We're either uncertain because the drive isn't strong enough to decide either way, or we know that whatever it is we 'should' isn't really what we *want* to do. There is often a comfort, some kind of an attachment, or strong sense of obligation, to the current situation.

If we're not prepared to either let them go, or work to fulfil them, then we must accept that these 'maybe' situations are probably going to hang around for a while, until something changes, and we have to be OK with that and live with any consequence.

For example, my weight-loss '5' - I want to lose 7lbs, but I'm not unhealthy, it's not a big enough problem for me to change my diet and exercise more on a regular basis.

It doesn't affect my life enough to be more of a yes. Would it be sensible and probably easier to modify my diet and exercise now, rather than later? Yes. Am I motivated to? No.

I must then accept that I want to be where I am, accept the consequence that I'm going to stay overweight, and that I might put on more weight if I do nothing.

Are you willing and prepared to accept the consequences of doing nothing about your middle-ground 'maybe's?

Whatever choice is made, whether we decide to change it, do it, let it go, or live with it, we must take full responsibility for that choice.

What's the point in 'should-ing' and feeling rubbish and guilty about it, but not doing, or saying, anything to change it? I have worked with several people who were in a horrible job situation, feeling attacked or ignored by people at work – but they never actually *told* those people that there was a problem, or that they wanted their ideas heard … how is the other person supposed to know if you don't tell them?

We all have a different perspective and if you don't change yours, or let other people know yours and therefore, change *their* awareness – the situation will stay the same.

If you accept responsibility for your status-quo until you are ready to WANT it more, or ready to let it go without guilt, then you put yourself in a more powerful position in relation to that 'should'. You are accepting it and CHOOSING to live with it in limbo for now.

Take a look at any of your 'maybe's but especially the 4 & 5's and ask yourself this:

"Can I happily take this 'should' off my list?" - Yes? Then let it go.

'No'? Then ask:

"Am I OK with doing nothing about it for now?" AND "Can I do nothing and not feel bad about it?"

If 'Yes' – then get on with your life.

If 'No', then look at it again, maybe you want to do it more than you think?

Set yourself a date to come back and look at it again – say in an hour or so, tomorrow, next week, or three months time – depending on the task of course: If it's "I don't want to do the washing up", three months may have some interesting consequences … but that is your choice of course!

A regular re-assessment of your should/want list is a great cleanser, as lives, circumstances, and mental head-space change from day to week to month.

What seems like a duty one day can become a desire the next: and visa-versa.

There will come a time when you think "that's been there a LONG time, am I actually going to do this thing, or not?"

Try looking at the 6 & 7's in the same light as the yes's … "What do I need to do to make that 6 a 7, or 7 an 8, what's standing in my way?" Then ask again – 'Do I really want it?'

You can also use the techniques in the upcoming 'no' section for your 'maybes' to turn those 'duty' shoulds in to a want 'desire'. This is especially useful if there are shoulds that are there out of a feeling of obligation, 'have to', or because they affect other people.

Tough choices ..

The No's (1-3)

We now come to the 'No's.

In some cases, this is as simple as: discovering you don't 'want' whatever it is, choosing to free yourself from it, and deciding NOT do it. Bin it. Ditch it. Gone!

By doing this you free up space in your life for something else.

It might be that it's something you used to want, it's there on your list out of habit and it's now become a should because you and others expect it of you. However, it's not actually your dream or goal any more, OR, it was never *yours* in the first place, it was something other people wanted for, or expected of, you.

Maybe some of these 'No's feel like they're an obligation, a 'have to' – like an invite to an event that you don't really want to go to. How would it feel to simply make your apologies and not go?

If you feel **relief** at making a 'No' choice (or any choice for that matter) ~ it's probably the right choice for you.

"Ahhhhh RELIEF!!"

In my book relief is the best emotion as an indicator of how you feel about saying yes or no to a choice you need to make.

If you feel the weight of the world shifting off your shoulders when you think about letting something go, or taking action to change something (it's often a letting go that creates relief) or a general sense of ease – then go with it.

The relief indicator is a strong tool to use, to discover if you really do, or don't, want that thing in your life.

Letting go of 'should' ... release that weight off your shoulders

Obviously, if your 'should' is something that affects other people, or is a massive life-shift, like quitting your job, then factor that in. You probably don't want to leave yourself in the mire with no money, or maybe that's a choice – to experience having nothing.

Make a plan of how to let it go, or create it, that plan may well take time; but remember that feeling of relief and you'll keep your motivation flowing.

Consequences & Choices: Turning "Should" into "Want"

If we're holding tightly to a 'no', a 'don't want to', rather than binning it – it's often because of the consequences.

Luckily, we can use the consequences to help us make choices – like my burning in the sun:

"I *should* cover up". Do I want to cover up? No.

I want to keep feeling the heat of the sun on my skin, it's March, I'm in Morocco! BUT the consequences of not covering up are that I will burn and be in pain – so I change the 'should' feeling to a consequence question:

"Do I want to be in pain?" a very simple NO, this fair, Irish, skin of my father's that I wear has burnt and turned me in to a lobster too many times.

So now I'm looking at a different situation: what do I want *more*? Rather than begrudgingly thinking to myself "I know I should cover up" I now ask, "How do I not burn?" So, I give myself options (the sunscreen isn't working) so I can:

1) Go inside

2) Put up a sun-brolly

3) Cover up

What do I choose?

Inside is dull and away from my friend who I'm on holiday with (this is my inner 13yr old feeling ostracised from the fun by being-inside-so-I-don't-burn "Boring")

The brolly also cools things down and I'm loving the warmth.

Or, I can stay where I am and cover up with a cotton shirt.

In the end, I find I *want* to cover up, because that way I can stay by the pool, with my friend, in the sun, and not burn.

NOW do I want to cover up? Yes! There has been a successful transformation from 'Should' and "No" – to 'Want' and "Yes"!

My choice is no longer a stroppy, child-like, 'should' choice that I'm going to begrudge – it's a positive solution to an immediate problem.

Breaking down your 'shoulds' and transforming them in to a 'want' means that ultimately, it's very rare that you then make a begrudging choice; you make a genuine decision to do something that gives you an outcome you desire.

My 'cover up' should may seem trivial, but it's an example of a simple way to start changing your mind-set around your shoulds.

Choices may be about what you DON'T want, more than what you do. This works because most people are more likely to move away from pain than towards pleasure.

I didn't want to be in pain *more* than not wanting to cover up.

It's a great way to tackle those every-day jobs that we get bored of, feel we 'have' to do, or which may have been hanging around for a while.

Like doing the laundry, gardening, cleaning, paperwork, going to the dentist, cooking for the children, whatever it is – ultimately, if you don't do the laundry you'll end up wearing dirty clothes and smelling.

I would rather do the washing than wear dirty clothes and smell! I'd rather do it NOW, so it's done, and I can crack on with what I really want to do.

However, if I was homeless, I would probably choose to spend whatever money I had on food, rather than doing the laundry, because that might be my choice. I wouldn't want to smell, but I'd rather eat.

(Remember the Viktor Frankl quote from earlier? He was in both Auschwitz and Dachau, sometimes we may not have great choices available to us, but we always have some choice.)

What choices can you make about your 'should's?

Look at your list and think about how you can start letting go of what you don't want in your life, how you can go about creating your yes's, and how you can break down your maybe's and the no's you can't let go of, to create more desire and want to do them.

Should = begrudging, heavy

DUTY

Want = positive, light

DESIRE.

To help you with this, take a few moments and, on another piece of paper, answer these questions in relation to each of the shoulds that you're still holding on to.

- What results will you get when you 'want' this instead of feeling you should?
- What will you create in your life that isn't there at the moment?
- How will that be worthwhile for you? (Even if your result is the relief of getting a nagging job done, or completing something that's been hanging around).

How do you feel now about making that choice?

I know that breaking down some of your shoulds may feel challenging to start with, but there is something quite tiresome about being a begrudging 'Should-er' who is always "doing your duty" because you feel it is expected of you.

How often do you find yourself wasting time complaining about some of the things on your list or in your life?

How much better does it feel to *want* to do something?

For example; visiting an elderly relative, or friend of the family, who is on their own, can feel like a duty that one 'should' do ….

OR; we could ask ourselves;

"If that's me when I'm old, would I want visitors?"

I would probably think:

'Yes, I don't want to be lonely and I don't want them to feel like that either'

or if they're frail,

'I might not see them again and I want to know I made the effort.'

So now I WANT to, I choose to. It makes *me* feel better to let them know that they are thought of, and cared for enough, to make the effort.

Whenever I feel 'should' energy creeping in at the edges, when I hear myself thinking 'I should', or feeling like 'I have to' I have, over time, trained myself to notice those thoughts, stop, and assess my WANT or DON'T WANT levels.

Sometimes I need reminding. When I catch myself complaining about 'having to do' something, feeling like I 'should' or, heavens forefend!! if the 'should' word creeps out of my mouth, then I give myself a sharp reminder – "THERE IS NO SHOULD, JUDITH … MAKE A CHOICE!"

This may happen with things you agree, or want, to do to start with, but then they start to feel like an obligation.

For example, trips away with friends or family - how often have they been arranged with, or by, others and you may initially want to go, but life circumstances have changed and then you've caught yourself adding them to a list of 'tasks that have to be done'?

I know I have done this with parties, hen-dos, weekends away, nights out; things I agreed to, then when it comes to the date all I really want to do is have a bath and an early night! But then you can choose to change your mind and drop out, or remember why you said yes in the first place, think of the good things about it and make a choice to want to do it – and enjoy it a lot more than begrudgingly going.

Or longer-term, maybe you say yes to something as a favour, or because you feel strongly about it at the time, or think it's a one-off, or won't take much time; and suddenly it's become your responsibility and you're arranging someone's whole wedding, or sitting on a committee for years, or running a stall at an event every year... whatever it may be, but you now no longer want to do it …. Remember, you don't have to.

"But I HAVE to" – Obligations & Objections

What if your 'Should/Want' list includes things like in the previous examples, things that might affect other people, or yourself, and you don't want to do, be, or have it, but feel like you *really* should? You HAVE TO.

'Have to' sounds like an obligation, it feels heavy, and full of responsibility and lack of choice.

"I have to go to work"

"I have to go to a wedding"

"I have to do the housework"

"I have to have a better car"

"I have to be the sensible one"

"I have to take care of the children"

No, you don't.

You can treat 'have to' exactly the same way you treat 'should' and find a way to want it, change it, delegate it, or let it go.

Decide what you want *more*; to do it, or not do it, to change it, or to live with it as it is.

Take a look at the consequences, make a choice and decide to "want" one thing more than another. Re-assess the importance of what you want, as well as the shoulds and have tos, and decide how much time, money, or effort you want to give each of them.

If you want to find time to paint, write, exercise, learn a language, not get overwhelmed, sleep, change your job, start a new business, whatever it is you "don't have the time" for – what is it you currently feel like you 'have' to do that can be re-assessed or re-arranged?

Do you clean the house every day? Does it have to be done *every* day? Would the world fall apart if you didn't clean, say twice a week, so you could fit in your other activity?

Is it possible to get up an hour earlier? Schedule your day differently? Make space somewhere? Let go of something else for what you want to do more? Give responsibility for some of the tasks you do at work or at home, to someone else?

Is it possible to ask for help?!! (This is a personal one, something I'm slowly getting better at.)

Yes, some choices might have a bigger effect on you than others and some might have to be discussed with other people and involve big changes, but how much do you want to reduce your obligations and increase your wants?

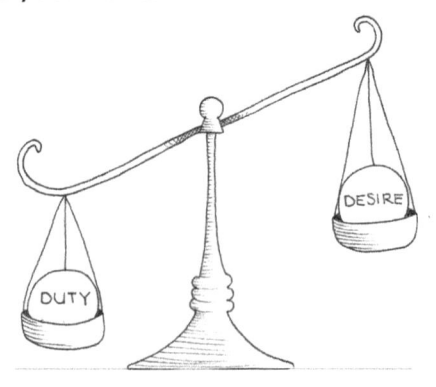

Exercise 2:
Changing or Letting Go of the Low-Score Wants

Take a look at each should on your list that scores under 6.

Now take five minutes and write down the answers to this question:

- "What are the consequences if I don't do (be, or have) this?"

Make sure you list all the potential consequences for each one, remembering to include both beneficial and potentially detrimental consequences, for both you and those others who this choice may affect.

Then:

Return to each item and score it a "yes" or "no" as to whether you are willing to suffer the consequences of binning this should:

If the answer is 'Yes' – if you are willing to suffer any detrimental consequences, or want the beneficial ones, then it looks like you don't want that should in your life – it's probably time to go ahead and take it off your list.

How does thinking about that feel? RELIEF...?

If it's simple to do so, then make that choice to stop doing whatever it is and take it out of your life.

If this 'should' is a big thing in your life, how you approach changing or removing it from your list may be a deeper process than this book. It may be that it's an important job - can you ask someone else to do it? It may be that you need a plan that is long term, or involves others. Find what works for you and set wheels in motion to reduce or remove this should from your life.

If making this plan, or these changes, is too much for you to do on your own, then find someone who can help give you clarity and support on your choice, a coach, mentor, friend or partner, for example.

If the answer is 'No', if you're not willing to suffer the consequences of deleting this should from your life, then how can you turn that 'should' or 'have to' into a want?

What questions can you ask, or choices can you give yourself, in order to create a 'what I want more' decision to make?

Always write down the answers to your questions, preferably by hand, on paper, but type it if that's easier. Just don't do it in your head; when we write something manually we solidify the thought and relate to it more strongly.

If you need some help, here are some starter questions:

- What are the positive results if you do this thing? List them.
- How will those results make you feel? Write that down.
- What effect will that have on your life? Write it down.

Are those results enough to make it a 'want'?

a) Yes? Ok.
b) No? Then what question can you ask, or choice can you make, to give yourself a 'what I want more' decision to make?

If there's still no 'want' – what needs to change?

Can you let it go?

What other questions would be useful for you to ask?

Who can you go to, or find, to assist you?

"I can't take this off the list – it will affect others too much"

If you've hit a wall and these shoulds you're looking at affect other people, and that's what's stopping you, try answering these questions:

- Which people does it affect?
- How does it affect them?
- On a scale of 1 – 10, how much do you care about these people?
- On a scale of 1 – 10, how much do these people care about you? (Go for truth not perception!)
- Are these other people's lives your responsibility?
- If you become happier as a result of not doing your should, how does that affect others?
- If you were to let them know how you feel about your should, how might they be able to help you?
- Who can you go to, or find, to help you?

Hopefully the answers to these questions will help you work around your beliefs about other people, find support from other people, or start to look at your challenges from a different perspective.

DON'T FORGET:

We all need to take responsibility for our own choices. We need to be aware that the action we take is a choice made in order to change a situation, or create a result we want.

Our actions, choices, and the words we use, sometimes don't create the result we expect or desire, alternatively; they may happen, but not in the time-frame or with the results we had hoped for, and we have to be happy to live with that too!

You might not be able to decide on your own.

If your shoulds feel too big, if you think it's not possible, or believe you don't have the resources or ability to do it, if you believe that other people will get in your way, or that whatever it is you no longer want to be 'shoulding' will affect others, or what you really want to be doing will get in the way of others' lives...

Then find help.

This is about finding your inner voice, learning to listen to what it is you really want to be doing, being, having, saying, living, in your life. If you have lots of 'noise' going on in the background in the form of your shoulds, then how will you be able to express your wants?

So, find help.

Engage those around you, talk to the people it affects, get a coach, find a specialist, possibly a therapist, look for someone who's done something similar and ask for advice (but remember that what's right for them might not be right for you and what was wrong for another might be your path to delight)!

Remember, you don't have to do anything on your own, but whatever you do ... make it a choice.

***Making Choices ... not always easy –
but find help and start sorting***

The reversie 'Should' ... ' SHOULDN'T'

This exercise is to give you a change of perspective. Our brains all work differently, some people will beat themselves up about the things they "should" do, others about those they "shouldn't" (the guilt factor) and for some of us it's a combination.

SO, what about those pesky 'Shouldn't' thoughts?? Are they there for you too?

"Oh, I really *shouldn't* have that extra glass of wine/chocolate/cake (chocolate cake)! /affair" OR "...buy that pair of shoes/ holiday/suit, turn over and go back to sleep ...".

My answer to this? Put simply and maybe somewhat harshly:

Then DON'T do that thing and don't complain that you're denying yourself.

Or, DO if you want to, but then don't go on about it because you feel guilty.

Take responsibility for your choices.

Unfortunately, it doesn't always feel that simple. Often our 'shouldn'ts' are related to things we enjoy, or that give us a brief endorphin kick.

Is your 'shouldn't' a reversed 'should'?

"I shouldn't eat so much rubbish" can be an inside-out version of "I should eat more healthily".

"I shouldn't waste so much time", might be a reversed "I should manage my time better" or "I wish I could create more time"!

Are you a 'shouldn't' person?

What motivates you more?

"I should lose weight" OR "I shouldn't be this weight"?

Looking at the above, which one do you create more compelling reasons from? Which one is easier for you to make a choice from?

It really doesn't matter, use whichever form works best for you, it may well be a mix. This is all about making a choice and taking responsibility for those choices and, ultimately, your life.

Whether you are feeling like you 'should' or 'shouldn't', getting rid of either is about making a choice.

This is about finding the easiest way for you to create a 'want', to make a choice that you are happy with and will act on.

For example, if "I don't want to be overweight" works better for you than "I should lose weight" then use the one that works better for you!

If you have shoulds on the list that you wrote earlier that you're still uncertain about, or not motivated to take action on, ask yourself if they would work, or motivate you, better, as a 'shouldn't'??

Try reversing them! See if it helps.

Exercise 3: "I Shouldn't"

Let's try it now …

Take your shoulds from before and reverse them. If you find it really too challenging to reverse them, see how I changed mine.

If I were to do mine they might look like this:

"I shouldn't …"

1) Be the weight I am
2) Turn on the internet when I want to write
3) Keep letting other projects distract me from my writing
4) Still be occasionally sleeping with my ex!
5) Stay in the sun

Do you see how making mine a 'shouldn't' has helped me get really quite specific and refine the problem for a couple of my 'shoulds'? Converting these to shouldn't, numbers 2 & 3 scream at me "I need to focus more"

Alternatively, why not create a new top 5 things you think of, that you feel you 'shouldn't'? Sometimes looking at things in this way highlights a different area of your life or lifestyle.

"I shouldn't …"

1) ……………………………………………………….

2) ……………………………………………………….

3) ……………………………………………………….

4) ……………………………………………………….

5) ……………………………………………………….

Has your list of shouldn't's brought up any useful ideas or things you might be able to implement so that you can create your 'want's?

If you created a new list for this exercise, are any of them connected to your 'shoulds'?

Here we go, tear out this page and take it with you so you can compare as we move on - or if you can't do the tearing thing …. write the above on a new sheet of paper!

Are any of your shouldn'ts obvious wants?

My numbers 2 & 3 become a clear want:

"I want to focus more in order to be more creative"

Number 4 as a 'shouldn't' seems to invite being opened out into a potentially longer sentence by adding "because"

"I shouldn't still be occasionally sleeping with my ex, *because* as fun as it is, it's not healthy for either of us, or helping us move on"

Do any of your 'shouldn't's open out to give you reasons why?

"I shouldn't *'x' because 'y' number of effects that has on my life*".

So, how is your original list looking now?

How did the reversing exercise affect your 'shoulds', are they becoming more specific? What difference might it make to your life?

Take a moment to look at your lists.

- Which 'shoulds' are you already taking action on, even if only in your mind?
- Which 'should's are you choosing to bin?
- Which ones are you going to live with for a while, not beat yourself up about, and come back to at a later date?

18 months after writing it in the first draft for this book; the list I wrote for these exercises now looks like:

1) **Lose 7lbs** – Achieved! But not until about a year later when, at 16lbs over where I like to be, it became a 10 want.

2) **Write this book** – Achieved! It went from a 10 on holiday to a 6 or 7 back in life "because of time restrictions". It became a 10 again when I was going through a bit of a 'blip', I MADE the time (getting up early and writing for an hour first thing, then doing edits in the same time slot, or on train and tube journeys.)

   It then sat for nearly another year as my business went through massive transition & finally, at the end of 2017 (having had the spark of the idea in 2015) I put the first version out to the world and now here you are reading it!

3) **Finish my play** – it's now a 5, I'm living with it not getting done until my business frees the time for me. I regularly assess whether to keep it there or not.

4) **Stop occasionally sleeping with my ex-boyfriend** Achieved!

5) **Cover up (so I don't burn)!** – Went from a 2 'no' to a 10 want in 5mins. Achieved!

Weight loss – in a survey I did, this came out as the number one 'should' that people have.

Lots of people feel they should lose weight, or "shouldn't eat or drink so much… (*insert indulgence of choice here.*)"

This is something that had been on my list for a while, the 'I should lose some weight' should; but it had to *really* start affecting my head before I took action.

When I reached 11.5 stone (161lbs, or 73kgs) my want became a 10. I ate better, exercised more - lost all 16lbs and am now happily balanced between where I want to be (10st 4lbs) and a maximum of 7lbs over that.

My biggest aid to staying with the weight loss? I took this photo, on my phone, of the scales at 16lbs over where I like to be and made it my phone screen-saver.

Every time I checked the time on my phone I was reminded of why I was changing my patterns. If I thought "I'm peckish, what time is it"?– there it was, I would see it and think "what do I want more"?!...

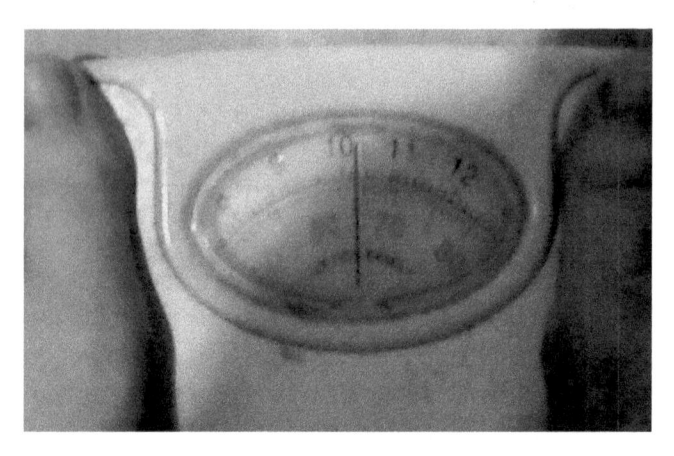

...I wanted to get to here more – 10st 4lbs! ...I now happily hang around the 10st 7lbs area (that's 147lbs or 65Kgs if you're not British!) When I find myself creeping back towards 11stone ... I take a look at if I've stopped exercising, or am eating more rubbish, then I take another picture and put it back on my screen saver.

The first picture was my screen saver for a long time after losing the weight – we have MASSIVE heart issues on both sides of my family and a tendency to 'get comfy' – I liked the reminder.

What practical reminders or things can you do to help you achieve your want?

Have a look at your list of wants and see if there's anything you can start implementing, or any simple reminders or tools you can create to keep you motivated.

Write them down!

"Congratulations!"

You are making choices,

You are making changes,

You are taking responsibility

And

You are starting to listen to your inner voice.

Ready for
the next step?

Turn the page.

Part 2
'Shoulding' Your Life

PART TWO

Your Life-Shoulds.

(Where your social voice comes from, or what it is restricted by).

In this next section of the book we'll be looking more deeply at the big shoulds that we live and where those "shoulds" come from. These are often partly where we either formed judgments around, or suppressed, our natural inner voice. (This is what I sometimes refer to as your social voice).

Most of the examples I use in this section refer to my acting career, as this is where I have felt the effects of 'should' the greatest. Often I found myself doing what I thought I 'should', rather than the things that might have helped me create what I truly desired.

If I'm honest, I wish coaches had existed when I was making a lot of my acting career choices, or that I knew of coaching, and that I would have had the mindset to pay for one. If I'm *really* honest, actors are almost as tight-pursed as backpackers, so the likelihood of me paying for a coach even if they had existed would have been slim. (This is often because actors are regularly not paid for a lot of work, jobs done in the hopes of 'being spotted', either that, or pay is low and life in London is not cheap.)

Obviously (and thankfully!) not everyone in the world is an actor, but I'm sure you have similar situations in your life that you can relate to, as your point of reference, as we go along.

Often these 'life-shoulds' surround the things we wish we had done, done more of, done differently, or are currently doing or living and wish we weren't.

How many times have you taken stock of your life and compared yourself to others, to what you feel you should have, or where you expected to be in life, and been disappointed with where you are, or found yourself lacking?

For whatever reason, society seems to put a lot of stock in certain age milestones; turning 16, 18, 21, 30, 40, 50, 65 all seem to have certain expectations linked to them, which we often take as "Shoulds". It's not surprising so many people go through a mid-life crisis and people now also talk about a quarter-life crisis. Crisis is not good – so let's try and avoid it.

Turning 30 for me (well over a decade ago now!) wasn't filled with any fear or, indeed, anything other than an excuse for a big party .... But about a year later, I remember walking home from one of my several promotion jobs (those people who stand on the street corner and try to give you a flyer, or free packet of tissues, or new product, are mostly out of work actors and dancers – so please be nice to my tribe!)

I was about to walk up the hill to my bedsit and as I looked up the literal hill I had to climb to get home I was overwhelmed with an immense sense of failure, and burst in to tears.

I was thinking:

"I'm 31. I have nothing".

Then I started really digging a pit for myself as I continued:

"I have no relationship, let alone marriage or kids, I live in a one-room rented bed-sit, my longest relationship didn't even make a year, I have no-one to share my life with. I'm working five different dead-end jobs to make ends meet, earning crap money trying to make my acting career work, which is going no-where. I don't even have an agent. I'm a failure."

The metaphorical hill I had to climb to get to where I thought I **should** be felt overwhelming and way too big.

The bedsit was one room, about 9' x 12', with a bed under the eaves with sagging wallpaper, a wardrobe, a desk and kitchenette, and there were two shared bathrooms between the residents of all 12 bedsit rooms in the house.

In order to pay the rent and have the flexibility to support being an actress I was on the books of several promotions companies, spraying perfume in department stores, private tutoring English, occasional corporate role-play acting work and even more occasionally an unpaid creative acting gig in the desperate hope someone from the industry might see & like me and give me that break[3]!

I'm aware that for some people my circumstances would be considered luxurious, I had a roof above my head and food in the fridge – I had a fridge to put food in. Don't get me wrong, I loved that bedsit, but it's not where I had expected or hoped to be.

The trouble with me on that day was that I wasn't living up to what I thought I *should* have, or *should* have achieved, by that point in my life.

I compared myself to others, strangers, friends and family:

"By the time my mum was my age she had been married twice, ran her own business with my dad, had two children and in a year and a half would have her third – what have I got"? or

"Sixteen-year olds have had longer relationships than me" or

"Maybe my English teacher was right, and I don't 'have the figure for acting', it *is* a stupid profession and I'm daft to be trying, I should just give up".

Where in your life do you have these kinds of thoughts? What is it that makes you want to just give up?

---

[3] For those not in the know, this is the reality for *most* actors ... it's not the exciting profession you think it is!

Worse than comparing myself to others ... I was comparing myself to what I had hoped I would be, and have, by the time I was thirty-something.

I'd always said that if I was going to have children I wanted the last by thirty because I'd seen how tired my mum got – and there I was having not even had a relationship that lasted longer than a year.

I'd wanted to be a successful (read regularly working & paid) actress, but I'd only been out of drama school three years and most of my work had been schools tours, unpaid fringe theatre, or awful student short films. (In their defence I was also yet to hone my screen acting skills and I was pretty shocking on screen! I hope those aspiring filmmakers learnt as much as I did!)

In my mind I SHOULD have been acting regularly and being paid for it, sharing my life with a man and at least thinking about the possibility of children.

I was looking at what I *didn't* have, but felt like I should, and comparing myself against what other people had and wondered what was wrong with me that I didn't.

When we compare ourselves, we tend to do so in comparison to those who we perceive to have more or 'better' than us. Where do you do this is your life? How does it help?

I'm not sure how long this phase lasted for me, but at some point I realised that what I was feeling was 'should-ing' "I should have", "I should be", "I should feel"...

I realised that although for seven years I'd been successfully and regularly getting rid of, or adjusting, my 'shoulds' when it came to actions (going to this, or doing that, or buying the other) I still had very firm 'life shoulds'.

So, after a while of self-pity, lingering in misery, I took a long hard look at what I was feeling "I should" have in my life and who I 'should' be as a person and re-adjusted my settings.

After all, no matter how much I felt 'should', no-one was going to give me those things – I had to figure out if I *wanted* them, then what I was going to do, or change, to create them in my life!

I didn't actually know this as a coaching process at that point in my life, but I knew I had to do something differently because no-one else was going to take care of my life for me.

Then I got a wake-up call from The Universe.

The Wake-up Call.

I had something massive come and knock me down out of the blue – my aunt, who I adored, suddenly died. I wasn't in the country, it wasn't expected, she was only 60, and we never got to have that 'girls together' day in town that we talked about on our last phone call.

There's nothing like a mortal wake-up call to help you look at your life and get re-assessing. I'm not sure why so many of us wait for these 'wake-up calls' but it seems we do. They take many forms, accident, illness, death, divorce, redundancy, being some of the most obvious – but things like promotion, marriage, buying a home, or getting pregnant, can also throw up a big 'reality check' flag.

Do you need to wait for a big wake-up-call to take a different look at your life, or have you already had one, which is why you're reading this?

If you've not had a life-shift happen yet, I'd like you to ask you something:

"What it would take to make you look at how you *want* to be living and take action to change it?"

Write that thing down. If there is more than one answer, write down all the things that could happen that would make you start taking action.

Do you really want to wait for that to happen?

How about, rather than waiting, we keep ourselves awake now, together, so we don't need to wait for the disaster to strike.

Life-Shoulds

Your life-shoulds are the things that you feel you 'should' be as a person, or be doing and have in your life, by now; milestones not reached, goals unattained, or maybe even dreams shelved.

Like my moment of looking up the hill, feeling like I should have been more successful, in a relationship, more secure, more established; do you have that feeling in your life? Have you had that feeling in the past?

Think about that time now, whether it is your current state, or something you've experienced previously. That feeling like you're not where you either should, or want, to be, don't have the things you 'should', or aren't the person you should be.

Take a moment to visualise the situation for me, feel what it feels like physically and emotionally, hear what it sounds like. What are people around you saying? What is the voice inside your head saying? What are you thinking? What do you think other people are thinking about you?

In this moment, or that time in the past, were/are you living YOUR life, is your inner voice being expressed in the way that you live?

Or are you standing at the bottom of that hill, looking up and feeling overwhelmed, unfulfilled, failed, or obliged by other people or powers-that-be, in some areas?

These life-shoulds tend to make themselves more known in reflective moments, or when we're discontented in some way. After-all, when we're deliriously happy we don't think that much about our 'don'ts' and 'not-have's!

What life-shoulds are you living by, or waiting for?

Your life-shoulds might be something you are LIVING. That is, you are living a should that you never really wanted but are doing so because others expect, or expected, it of you. Perhaps you are in your job because you felt you 'should' do that – you don't really want to be a doctor, accountant, teacher, service advisor, shop assistant, whatever you are - you wanted to be an artist, vet, musician, clown, train driver, nurse. Maybe you have children and feel you 'should' have a stable life - but what you want is to be travelling the world.

Maybe it's the other way round and you feel no-one ever really expected anything of you, you 'shouldn't' expect to do, or become, anything – and you've accepted that and put your desires on the shelf to 'get by' and 'survive'.

The 'being' life-shoulds are often long-held beliefs about ways you should behave, or things you believe you should be living up to – often in order to get a response from the significant adults in your life from childhood. Common ones are beliefs like:

"I should be successful" (To get acceptance or recognition)

"I need to be strong" (To protect, or make life easier for, others)

"I should 'be good', 'be kind' or 'be nice'"

The last examples seem to come with an undercurrent of "I shouldn't 'be difficult'", "I shouldn't make waves for others", or "I shouldn't contradict or 'rock the boat'".

Unfortunately, this can also end up as "I shouldn't express my frustrations, anger, disappointment; or any emotion, thought, or idea that might contradict, upset or annoy others" ... not great for listening to your voice, or for self-expression, going for what you want, asking for what you need, or speaking up for yourself.

Exercise 4:

On the next page, or a new piece of paper, write down up to five big old life-shoulds. If you have a life-should or two on your other list too, that's OK you can use them here as well because we're looking at them in a slightly different way, and who knows, it might help you get some clarity on them.

If it helps – my life-shoulds on an 'off' day might read (or have read in the past):

I should……

1) Be, or have been, in at least one, proper, long-term relationship by now

2) Have a 'steady' job

3) Have a pension

4) Be a more successful actress, or give up!

5) Be happier

"I should …."

1) ....
2) ....
3) ....
4) ....
5) ....

Whose Shoulds Be These?

Having looked at some of your life-shoulds, it's time to look at where they come from. We are going to take things one step further and ask:

"Whose 'shoulds' are they?"

Are these shoulds and beliefs *yours*, or are they absorbed from, or handed down to you, by other people?

What can you do, or how can you look at things, to be easier on yourself?

For example, did I really want to be married, with kids and a 'normal' job when I was standing at the bottom of the hill, or did I feel that is what was expected of me because that's what *most* people do?

Or, was I just overworked, under fulfilled, out of money and lonely? (I'll give you a clue … it's not the first option)!

Let's look at another way to either turn those 'shoulds' into a want, discard, or disempower them.

Next step:

Look at each of your life-shoulds in turn and ask yourself the following questions:

"Does that come from me"?

If yes, write 'me' next to it.

If the answer is 'no' then ask yourself:

"Who wants, or wanted, that for me in my life?" or "Where did I get that 'should' from"?

Write down next to your should who, or where, it came from.

Next step:

Now, go back to the top and for each one, ask yourself:

"How long ago did I assume this 'should'?"

Write next to each 'should' *when* that 'should' came from, or if you prefer, what age you were when you started thinking or believing it.

It may well be that a should or belief of the past is one that belongs to you, but to a younger, different, you – you at 7, 15, 25, 50, or last week. It might have been a useful 'should' once, but it is no longer relevant or useful.

My example life-shoulds now might read:

I should……

1) Be, or have been, in at least one, proper, long-term relationship by now – **'Society' (and me) – since I was about 24**

2) Have a 'steady' job – **Seemingly all adults - since about 14**

3) Have a pension – **'Society' – people started asking when I was about 27**

4) Be a more successful actress, or give up! – ***Anyone* ever who I tell I'm an actor & me aged 17 / 27 / 30 … onwards…**

5) Be happier – **The world of advertising! – Since forever – (and now Facebook seems to be in on the game)**

Looking at your own life-shoulds, what stands out to you?

Some of these shoulds may have been helpful once, some may still motivate or inspire you, some may be big old blocks to finding or using YOUR voice, because they are someone else's beliefs.

What is important in your life?

Take a moment to look at your responses and ask yourself some of the questions below.

I'd suggest taking one life-should at a time and exploring it on a fresh page. Write down your answers to the questions that resonate, without over thinking them, just let whatever needs to come out be expressed.

The below are questions to spark your thought process if you need it – you don't need to answer each of them.

- Is, or was it ever helpful to hold, believe, or live that should?
- What are your beliefs about your life, about yourself and about other people in connection to this?
- What fears are there around what will happen if you don't live this should?
- What fears, beliefs or uncertainties are around pursuing your dreams?
- Who or what are you comparing yourself to?
- What is it that restricts, or restricted, you from taking action, or even thinking something is possible?
- Is it still relevant, or true for you?
- Is it true, or is it your perception of what you *think* other people expect?

What has come up for you from this exercise?

Often when we look in to what's behind our life-shoulds, there are fears or beliefs that limit or restrict us. You may have got the pattern by now, but often these fears and beliefs also don't belong to us, they come from parents, teachers, those we look up to.

These patterns are multiple, and include things like:

- Not being good enough, that is not living up to other people's (or our own) expectations, or fear of letting people down

- Not belonging, a fear of rejection (a mix of this and not being good enough is what I was feeling on releasing this book!)

- Not being worthy of a position or of taking a stance, or expressing an opinion

- Fear of failure, fear of success, fear of being negatively judged (this is a MASSIVE one when it comes to speaking and people always seem to forget that we can also be judged positively – how else do people win competitions?)

- Believing there's not enough of something (love, money, time, resources etc)

The list could go on, but you get the idea.

What are the **fears** behind your life-shoulds, and who or where do those fears come from?

Here are the beliefs and fears my example list brought up for me:

1) Relationship – **I will always be alone** – *a mix of my 'not good enough/don't belong' belief & reaction to my mum & dad's relationship.*

2) 'Steady' job – **I won't ever earn enough money to live without 'scrimping'** – *family fears for me*

3) Pension – **What if I end up old and penniless?** – *advertising & family*

4) Be a more successful actress – **Or I've failed -** *me, not wanting to lose face in defiance of those who told me I should do something more secure, basically me wanting to say "I told you so"!*

5) Happier – **Others will always have more than me** *(I think this would be relationship connected, so me)*

Even though most of these 'life-shoulds' are past for me, the core beliefs behind the fears are still very active. This is because our core beliefs are a part of who we are, they are rooted in our structures, the 'auto-response' we go to if we're not aware. Through a combination of the trainings I have done, I have learnt to recognise these beliefs so that when they come up I can re-focus, re-structure and respond in a more constructive way.

We ALL have core beliefs which can both benefit and challenge us. These beliefs don't have to mean anything, but it's useful for you to know that they're there and that they will show up in life. It's also useful to be able to use them to either create something new, or to voice it and say to yourself "That's a belief – it might not be true!" When we know what's stopping us, we can shift our perspective and look at the problem from a different viewpoint.

The next step is to take a look at your list and add whether or not your shoulds are something YOU want, and if they align with your values, with who you are and what you believe in.

So mine might have looked like this:

"I should....

1) Relationship - **Yes,** *I want & it aligns*

2) 'Steady' job – *Part of me would love to know how much money was coming in at the end of the month, have paid holiday, sick-pay, benefits, bonuses and people to talk to during the day and socialise with in the evenings - but really –* ***"Nope!"***

3) Pension – *I 'should' probably think about providing for my future* (so now we look at turning it in to a want)!

4) To act, or not to act?! - **Yes,** *I want to act ~ in part it involves other people making choices of whether I can or not – auditions are not entirely in my control* (so I need to look at my focus & actions – what I can do to help myself).

5) More happiness – *I'm pretty happy at the moment, but yes, I want more happiness but not the 'advertising' version ~ "What makes ME happy?" (Freedom, Connection & Creativity – my 3 big life-values) Also – learning that happiness is also a choice was a powerful lesson.*

What do your life-shoulds look like now? What do you think, or how do you feel about them?

Do you want these 'shoulds' in your life, do you want to convert them from a should to a want? Try scoring them from 1 – 10, like we did before and see which ones are left on your page (assuming you're going to bin or transform any under a 4).

Now that you know whether it's your, or someone else's, ideas you're thinking or living, and whether or not you actively want those 'shoulds' at this point in your life, you can start looking at them from a new perspective.

You can actually do this with your day-to-day 'shoulds' too – just because your mum cleaned the house thoroughly every day – do you have to? Just because your parents were teachers, do you have to be? Whose standards, or life, are you trying to live up to? Do you have the same values as them? Do you really want that lifestyle?

Say I was working as an executive PA in the city[4] because a 'steady job' is more secure, my family and I wouldn't have to worry so much about what income I've got coming in, and I wouldn't spend so much time on my own.

A 'steady job' would also tick the 'pension' (or future planning) box and, who knows, with a social life that comes with a 'normal' job (as opposed to multiple solo-self-employments) maybe even the 'relationship' one too.

However, although being an exec PA in the city was an option for me - I was offered a full-time 'proper job' (because obviously acting or the arts in general is not a proper job)! - it was never really a choice I was going to make, because acting was always stronger.

When I was offered that job, at 34, I was single, with no children and no responsibilities, with a huge passion for acting and a strong belief that we only really regret the things we really want to do in life, and don't (or don't try).

Oh, and, of course – I don't like "should". There was no way I could turn that steady-job 'should' in to a 'want' no matter how I looked at it.

---

[4] Been there, done that, as a long-term temp, am very good at it, but I chose not to take the full-time job offered because I wanted to be free to pursue acting.

I know I would have felt frustrated, unfulfilled and like I'd given up on myself if I'd have given up acting when the city career possibility arose.

I also may not have discovered coaching, started doing what I'm doing now, helping people find their voice and changing their lives, or written this book!

SO, when I've felt rubbish about where I am in life, I've had to take responsibility for the choice I made: I am responsible for the insecurity, lack of regular financial flow, uncertainty of employment and the moments of exasperation, despair and the roller coaster of emotions connected with a life in the arts and entrepreneurship.

Just because you are aware though, doesn't mean you don't feel the pressure of expectations!

Changing your perspective: Living a 'life-should' as 'want'

We are not all actors, or artists in the world. I use these examples as often the nature of that side of my life is the one that has come with the most 'should's attached.

What is in your life, or on your list, that feels like your version of the 'steady job'?

If you feel like you are living a 'should' – let's take the job as an example (it could as easily be a relationship, or state of being, or something else) how can you make it more of a want?

If you feel stuck in, or like you hate your job, but it pays you enough to live a certain lifestyle, or to survive, if it puts food on the table and pays the bills – is that actually enough for you to make it a want for now?

When you look at what that job (or other 'thing') provides you that is good and beneficial, is that enough to change your perspective?

Are you able to look at the 'life-should' in another way and make going to work in that job, being in that relationship, having (or not having) those children, owning that house, or whatever it is - a 'want'?

Although it may not be your 'dream' right now, does it fulfil a purpose at present, that you want *more* than to change your situation for now?

Does the life-should you're living support you as you go about creating what you want more? If it's not at the moment, how could it?

Now, let's be clear, if you're adapting the way you look at your life-should to make it more of a want, to make it easier to live with, this doesn't mean you take your true wants and dreams off your desire list and just put up with what you've got. I doubt you'd be reading this book if you were 100% happy with your life.[5]

Perhaps the life-should you're looking at is not serving you in any way, whether it belongs to someone else, or maybe once upon a time it was what you wanted. Now, though, it feels old and outdated, doesn't serve you anymore, and you want something different from life. If so, what is that something different that you want? (More security? More freedom? More fulfilment? More creativity? More health? ... the list of options could be endless.)

If you're tired of your life-should or it's become an out-dated 'want' I'm not suggesting that you just up-sticks and ditch your job, abandon your children, or stop aiming for a different way of life.

What I am suggesting is that you start changing the way you look at the 'should' you are living at

---

[5] Unless, of course, you're a friend, or family member, reading this out of a sense of 'duty' ... in which case I return you to the exercise 1 and put 'reading this book' on the list!!

the moment. From there, you can start getting creative about how to live, or create, what you really want.

Changing the Energy

In the same way that we can change our perspective of how we look at our shoulds, we can change the energy around how we think, talk about, or view something.

Feeling like you 'should' something has a begrudging, heavy, energy about it. To 'want' something feels lighter and more empowered. If you change the energy from a begrudging 'should' in to an empowered 'want', from duty to desire, whether that is a day-to-day should or a life-should, you then change what you get back from that thing.

This exercise helps you to remind yourself of the reasons why you're doing something; of your choices.

I could begrudge my uncertain, sporadic, overly-independent, sometimes isolated life – but I chose it in several ways, on several occasions, over my lifetime and I keep making choices every day to keep doing some things and to change others.

I have always lived MY life and reaped the rewards, and paid the costs, of that.

Look again at those life-shoulds that aren't yours, if you feel you do something out of obligation, or someone else's expectations, how can you change that?

Did you become a dentist, lawyer, teacher, builder, nurse etc – because that's what your parents did and you felt it was expected of you, or you were told it would be a good path, maybe it felt easier to do that, than do something else, to pursue your dream or buck the trend? Did you become what you are because you felt 'society' didn't give you a choice?

How could you look at your shoulds and see what they have given you?

How can you change the energy around them?

How can you create your wants from where you are?

Exercises Review

Before we go any further in to your shoulds, take a moment to see where you've come. Have a look at your 'should', 'shouldn't' and 'life-should' lists, what have you discovered about yourself and the life you are living?

What have you changed already?

What shifts are happening in your mindset?

Do you *want* to do those things on your lists, do they fulfil you? (If the answer is yes, then great – you've transformed duty to desire)!

If not:

What shoulds are not *yours* on your list(s)?

Who is it that thinks you 'should' do, be, have, those things? Do the same people recur?

If it *is* your should, what is stopping you making it a want?

If it is your *want*, that you're not doing, what is stopping you from fulfilling it?

Is it an *old* want or should? Are you hanging on to it either out of some kind of loyalty to a version of you that doesn't exist any more; or out of a determination that if you don't do it you will have 'failed'?

Did you want to become whatever it is that you are doing in life right now, or are you fulfilling other people's expectations of you?

Look at any should/wants that are left on your lists which either have a 'want score' of less than 7, or are not yours.

Take each one in turn and let me ask you this:

- What would happen if you didn't live, or do, that 'should'?
- What would you exchange it for?
- What's stopping you?

Take a moment to think about these and write your answers down.

Hopefully, by now you've already started to think about your shoulds and wants differently, you're feeling more connected to your inner voice and there are changes you've made and ideas sprouting. Hopefully you feel more confident in being able to express some of those things.

However, there may well still be some things there which are standing in your way, the reasons, the 'buts', the other people, the nagging thoughts that won't let you go: in other words, the blocks.

Part 3
"What's Stopping You?"

PART 3

WHAT'S IN YOUR WAY: THE BLOCKS

Sometimes, no matter how much we might want something, we just can't seem to find the way to make it happen. There are various reasons why this might be, social, financial, physical, mental, emotional....

This book is about finding your inner voice, discovering what it is you want. How you go about creating, achieving, or expressing that want … well....that's probably another book or two brewing, but if you can't wait for that, there's finding a coach, mentor, or friend to help you start living more of your wants.

However, there is something else that might help – and that is, starting to look at what those blocks between you and going for your desire are. What is stopping you from expressing and creating action around what you want?

Sometimes it could be as simple as, you believe it's 'selfish', or now is just not the right time – but that doesn't mean it shouldn't be there.

**What obstacles are getting in the way of your goals?
How can you break through them?
Get over them? Go around them?
Get under them?**

Reasons or Excuses?

When I catch myself feeling begrudgingly like "I have to" – which I *do* - I do exactly that, I *catch* myself, shift my perspective and make a choice.

Sometimes I don't catch myself …. and that's when things tend to go a bit flat, or challenging, in life; or completely pear-shaped and fall apart!

We need a compelling reason for making a choice. If it's not compelling enough, it might work for a while, but then you'll feel your energy change around it. This is why doing something purely for the money often doesn't work out; although it can be useful in the short-term, and life with it is easier than without, money is often not the biggest long-term motivator.

If you really *don't* want those shoulds on your lists in your life … then what's stopping you from changing them?

If you've shifted 'should' to 'want' and you really *do* want them, what's stopping you from creating them, or making them happen?

This is where the fears, beliefs and expectations that we were working on in the last exercise come in. Whether those beliefs belong to other people and you've appropriated them, or whether they are yours, they are powerful restrictors.

We have reasons and make up excuses (or make up excuses and call them reasons)! as to why we "have-to", or 'should', do something; or why we *can't* do something else.

Often these reasons are steeped in either your own, or someone else's, fears, beliefs, expectations, or judgements; OR your *perception* of other people's judgements, expectations, fears & beliefs.

This is where a lot of our 'life-shoulds' also tend to fall.

If you're a hoarder and you think "I should make some space" ~ but never do it.

If you feel "I should be more successful at my job/in my business" ~ but keep on doing the same thing year after year.

If maybe you "should keep in touch with friends better" ~ then another year goes by and you've not actually spoken to them.

Or, if like over 50% of the people who responded to my survey which asked: "*What are the top three things you feel you 'should' do, be, or have in life?*" you feel like you 'should':

"Eat more healthily", "Exercise more" or "Lose weight"[6] ~ but you are still eating rubbish, not getting fitter, or living life heavier than you want to.

If you're not doing it, maybe you don't *really* want to. If you say you *do* really want to, then I ask...

---

[6] 61 people responded: 50% gave one of those answers – 5 of whom gave two of those in combination

What's stopping you?

What are the reasons you're giving yourself – and are they actually excuses?

How much do you REALLY want that thing that you're saying you want? Are you trying, but banging your head against a brick wall of the same things that are stopping you every time? Have you tried looking at the challenge from a different angle?

The "Battle of The 'But's"

(and that's not J-lo vs Beyonce)!

What is the thing that is stopping you?

Is it because you're actually 'shoulding' those things rather than wanting, or figuring out how to want, then create, them?

Is it other people, or circumstances, that you feel are in your way? Or is it the voices of others, or in your mind, which keep you thinking that it's not possible?

Is it that you're fighting the battle of the 'buts'?

Sometimes it's easier to just leave things as a 'should' and complain about it.

Sometimes, having changed our should into a want, or discovering our wants some other way, we then have to face the battle of the things that stand in our way, or that *we* put in our way, or *think* are in our way....

"I want 'x' (insert desire of choice here) BUT..."

"But it's hard".

"But I don't have the money".

"But I don't think like that".

"But I don't have the time".

"But that's just who I am".

"But I'm not built for running" …. but … but …. but……

When we want something enough we will move mountains to make it happen ~ even if that means chipping one piece of the mountain out of the way at a time.

Sometimes we have to find a way of building something to go over the mountain, or finding a different way around it.

We'll do it even despite having those voices in our heads (or sometimes the voices of actual people) telling us that we can't, or shouldn't, or it's not safe, or not achievable.

When we want something enough, there are no 'but's.

When you look at your lists, what reasons for not doing those things do you give? Are those reasons yours, or have you picked them up from someone else?

Look at what's left on your lists and write down the obstacles that have stopped you from creating or doing those things in the past. These are your metaphorical mountains.

What mountain(s) do you have to move?

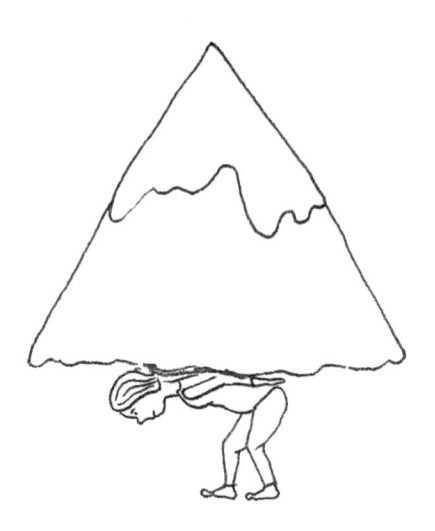

Is it a physical obstacle (money, people you're responsible for, paperwork, the location you live in, something else?)

Is it a mental one (uncertainty, thoughts and voices, nay-sayers, past perceived failures) making you think you can't?

Is it an emotional mountain (stuck in patterns created from feeling loss, overwhelm, despair, not good enough?)

Is it something else?

Is it even a mountain at all? Are your 'should'-based fears, beliefs, judgements and/or expectations changing your perspective of what might actually be a molehill?

Have a look at one of the things that is standing in the way of one of your wants. If it was a physical obstacle what would it be?

Describe the obstacle in detail: give it a size, shape, feeling, smell, sound. Is it a brick wall across your road of life, or is it a traffic-cone? Is it guarded by fierce dogs, an alarm bell, or by mythical ideas? Is it a mountain, or when you step away from being under it – is it really a mole-hill?

Is it as big a problem as you think it is?

How real are the challenges?

Can the obstacle be broken down in any way at all?

Is there a way you might be able to climb over it, create a ladder to get over it, one step at a time, or pick it up and throw it away?

"Oooh it's a tough profession"

The Voices of Doom

Sometimes our mountains (or molehills) are made up of the things we feel we 'should' do, be, or have, before we are able to achieve our wants. Sometimes people feel that they 'should' have the mountain, *rather* than the thing, or life, they actually want!

Other times those obstacles are there because we believe that our wants are selfish, not possible, out of reach, or unrealistic, for us.

These barriers often make themselves known as thoughts or voices from our life experience – but those thoughts or voices are not always our own. Often, they are ones we have appropriated from other people.

I call these "The Voices of Doom!"

For example, I didn't know how much other peoples' ideas, opinions, fears and beliefs would influence my actions in relation to my acting career.

"You should never be a penny in debt"

As a 15yr old I knew specifically what I wanted. I had a definite goal, a clear idea of what success would look like for me:

"No, I don't want to be 'famous' I want to work as an actress for a living and play Lady Macbeth at the Royal Shakespeare Company"[7]

What I *didn't* have was an awareness of goal setting, no clue about finding a mentor, or coach.

I also had no idea of just how much I would take on other people's beliefs and let other things get in the way.

"What good is a Drama & Theatre Arts Degree?"

I had no idea that I would listen to so many of 'the voices of doom!'

"Judith doesn't really have the figure for acting...has she considered the law? She'd make an excellent barrister"

This is what my English teacher said to my mum at parent/teacher night when I was 16!

My 'voices of doom' saw me try to avoid acting until I finally went to drama school at 27, which can be seen in the profession as kind-of late, or maybe not late enough.

---

[7] Shakespeare's Globe did not exist at the time ... I'm still available - all audition offers accepted!

Some voices of doom may be based on truths, some are opinion.

"I'm not different/ attractive/ slim/ quirky/ talented/ well-connected enough to do well"

I believed them all to some degree and being repeatedly told all this (mostly by people who had nothing to do with the profession) was not helpful, even if they did have my best interests at heart.

The people who told me all these things you're seeing – they cared about me and didn't want me to suffer the life of a financially struggling, out of work, actress.

"You'll need a proper job to fall back on"

Whose voices are stopping you?

What do you hear or feel when you think about some of the things on your lists?

Whose voice is telling you that you 'should' do something else first, or that you can't do, or shouldn't expect too much from what you want to create? (Or annoyingly both at the same time?)!

Exercise 5:
Your Buts & Voices of doom

This exercise is to discover what is stopping you from doing the things that you say you want to; so do this for those wants and 'shoulds' that you've converted to wants, which score over a '7'.

Start with one, maybe that which you have held the longest, maybe the thing you really want to do but haven't started, or don't believe you can.

1) What are your 'buts'? That is, what are the reasons/excuses you use for not doing things to create this?

2) What or who do you hear, feel, or know, as the reasons why you are either currently living a big 'should', or not creating the things you desire?

Now have a look and see if you can hear the 'voices of doom' and acknowledge:

- Who do they belong to? (It may be you or someone else. Are there repeat 'offenders'?)

- What is fact?

- What is fear? (yours or theirs)

- What is belief? (yours or theirs)

- What is judgement? (yours or theirs)

- What is expectation? (yours or theirs)
- Are the above helpful? Do they motivate you in any way?

Whether the voices or blocks are yours, or someone else's: name them, know them, write them down and have a look at your 'should' or 'want' in relation to them.

Do you still want to own those opinions, ideas or beliefs, or do you want to let them go?

Beware Blame!

Now that you are more aware of some of the sources of your 'shoulding' and 'Voices of Doom!' be careful not to go about blaming others for your life and choices.

This is really important.

People generally do, or say, things either out of their best intentions, or from their own fears. They don't *intend* to go around handing out hurt, limiting beliefs, restrictions, or emotional scars; people are too busy being focused on their own experiences. Remember, it's all perception – what you see as someone's anger, could be their frustration, or tiredness, what you see as their apathy or aloofness could be their fear of judgment, or timidity.

In the same way, you didn't *intend* to go around picking up those limiting beliefs and restrictions. It's really quite amazing how much humans will listen to, pick up on, create, or respond to, in relation to the voices of doom and how they leave any of the good comments and experiences behind.

Remember, ultimately, we must take full personal responsibility for our life choices, look at where they have brought us, celebrate the good stuff, hold on to the lessons learnt, and dump as much of the rest as possible.

If we are dissatisfied with where we are, then it's time to start making new choices, empowered by knowing that we are *now* taking active, aware, decisions.

It's handy, isn't it – having someone else to blame? How many times have you said or thought "I *knew* I shouldn't have listened to you."? REALLY? If you *knew* then why did you ask them? (Or were they just the Voices of Doom you were listening to?)

Although we may like to make excuses, and blame others, a lot of life challenges come down to our own perspective and focus.[8]

Returning to my acting example, my family knew nothing about acting and although they always gave their support and advice from a place of love, it also came from a place of ignorance of the profession (and possibly a fear that I'd spend my life being a penniless artist, starving in an attic somewhere – hmm – did I mention the bedsit!)

So then why did I ask my *mum* which of my two audition pieces I should do for a certain university?

I knew the two I thought I should do, but she said different ones and I went with them, and didn't get the re-call audition, let alone an offer of a place.

---

[8] **Please Note:** Obviously, there are some things that happen in life which are done *to* people, where blame is fairly apportioned. If you have lived a life where someone has abused their position over you then I hope the situation was dealt with and that you have found help to overcome that. If you haven't, please do – there are so many wonderful places to give support so that you can start making choices to live your own life, not one controlled by someone else's words or actions.

Why did I ask my mum?

- Because she saw them from the outside and I couldn't.
- Because I wanted support.
- Because at 17 I was already listening to so many of the voices of doom that made me feel like I'd never be good enough to 'make it' as an actress, that I already didn't trust myself.

I can't remember why I didn't ask my drama teacher, or someone who had a better idea of what the audition panel would be looking for; I think because I didn't believe he thought I could get in.

So instead, I spent years silently wishing I'd never listened to my mum, slightly resenting that I did, with thoughts like:

"I should have done the other piece first."

and

"If I'd done the other piece, I might have got the re-call, I might have had an offer and gone to that university, and my career would be different"!

... really? Would I? Would it?

Who knows? And how does thinking all that help me?

There's no point appointing blame because it was my choice in the end.

It may well be that I was just not good enough, or right, for them - even if I had done the other piece,

I may still not have received a place, or maybe I might have got in and still have had the same career and life-path.

How many times have you blamed other people or circumstances for stopping you from achieving your 'want' or keeping you in a 'should'?

("If only they had/hadn't done/said 'x'....").

How many times have you taken someone's well-meaning advice on something, only to hold it against them later if it didn't work out?

("If you hadn't told me to ....").

"It's All YOUR Fault"

Are you asking the right people? When your go-to person says "maybe you should try 'x' " do they know? Are they the right person to be asking that thing?

"I wish I had ..." and 'Should have's, are regrets. As you know, I solidly believe "You only really regret the things you really want to do, but don't".

Paradoxically, this is where 'should' can become useful, when it is in the past-tense, because you can phrase it as "what should/could I have done differently?" The next time you're in a similar situation you can give yourself some perspective, use your past experience and give yourself options.

If you don't have restrictions that come from others going on in your head, might the thing that's stopping you, possibly, in fact, be you?

EXERCISE 6

Like my old grudge that I should have trusted my instinct and not listened to my mum, how many past 'I should-have or shouldn't-have...' moments do you have in your life?

These are often the thoughts or experiences that you think might have made a difference to the way your life has turned out; often "The ones that got away" or they might start, "I wish I had... ".

How many are you holding on to that stop you from moving forward now?

What is stopping you from letting them go?

If you'll find it useful, write them down. Take a look at these regrets or 'should haves' and ask:

- How old are they? (if it's easier – how old was I when this happened?)
- How do they repeat in my life?
- What have I learnt from them?
- Is there anything I can do about them now?

Can you look at them now and laugh, or smile fondly and think 'ah well' ... if I'd done that I might not have done something else?

What can you do differently next time you're in a similar situation? What would you tweak, or adjust only slightly?

What would you never do again for a million wishes?

Those that you're still holding on to, is it time to let them go? If so, then what do you need to do in order to let them go?

Hopefully this process helps you develop your choices for the 'wants' that you've created from your previous 'should' lists. It may increase your 'want' score, or take you one step further towards letting go of, or changing, a 'should'.

Perspective & Focus

When we have a firm set of beliefs it means we come at something from a specific angle – and that is the perspective that colours everything else we look at in relation to the topic.

Again using acting as an example, I used to say "Acting's a shit profession", all the time; even before I had much experience of actually being in the business!

It was a belief that came from what everyone around me (mostly not in the profession) said, and from watching a couple of people I knew who were pursuing it, struggle.

However, "Acting is a shit profession" became my firm perspective and, in many ways, my expectation, because we see in life what we expect to see, and create what we believe.

If I'd looked for people thriving, could I have found them? Yes. Less of them, certainly, but they exist and there was one woman who is a very respected actress in the industry who used to be married to a guy at my amateur theatre group. Still, it's easier to hear and believe the masses, and I squashed myself with the beliefs from those voices of doom, turning them in to 'should's and have-to's and putting *them* before my career:

"I have to pay the rent first"

"I have to run my car"

"I have to not go in to my overdraft"

"I have to do it all on my own"

"I have to have another 'proper' 'money' job"

"I have to prove to everyone who's ever questioned acting as a career choice that I CAN make money as an actor, and survive with a reasonable quality of life!"

Of course, if I was putting these things first, then how was I working on my acting career?

I wasn't.

I wasn't keeping my focus on the one thing I really wanted because I was

> *"Letting 'I dare not' wait upon 'I would'"*[9] ....

In other words, I dare not really go for it 100%, I let the 'have to's take priority, and get in the way, of what 'I would', of my desire, of really going for my career.

So where was my focus?

---

[9] Lady Macbeth (1.7.44) – sorry – this literally just spurted out of me here!

My focus was more on:

"How do I SURVIVE[10] as an actor?" and "How do I show *them* I can be paid to act?"

Rather than:

"How do I create a successful acting career and get to the RSC to play Lady M?"

Instead of working towards my end goal, creating the path to the RSC (or The Globe!) I bounced around from low-paid, or low-professionally respected, acting gigs to prove to myself that 'I am an actress', to temp jobs to make money, grateful for any acting table crumbs that came my way.

Instead of focusing on the things I needed to do to create the best possible chance of the career I wanted, I was letting my voices of doom create my path by trying to prove to them I could 'be an actor' by taking the validation jobs – "Look I'm being paid to act" (even when those jobs didn't lead me to where I wanted to go)!

Where in life have you let your focus be distracted, even though you may have been sort of heading,

---

[10] The concept that we expect to 'survive' at best as actors is so prevalent a thought in the profession there is even an annual event called "Surviving Actors".
Admittedly, this belief is something that can be backed up by statistics from a survey the UK actors' union Equity took in 2013 where, of 3,500 respondents, 49% earned less than £5,000 from their professional work in the entertainment industry in the previous year, with one in five earning nothing whatsoever.

in vaguely the right direction? If you start listening to your inner voice, instead of to your voices of doom – where might you end up?

How could I have adjusted my choices to fulfil my desire?

Could I have turned down those acting jobs that weren't going to further my career and that took me away from London for months?

What might I have done with the time and money I *did* have? Or with what I might have had if I'd not taken the non-result focused acting jobs?

Taken classes? Written letters? Built contacts? Auditioned for unpaid plays that would get me seen? Created plays, or filmed sketches, to put on with others? Found support or help?

What could you do to adjust your choices and create your desires?

EXERCISE 7

Take a moment to look at some of your high-scoring wants and note how you look at them in your life: Take one at a time and answer some of the questions below:

What you are focusing on?

How do your life-'shoulds' colour your 'wants'? Do you look at your desires through a distortion of beliefs?

Are you looking at the other people who have failed at what you want to do, and how hard it is? Or are you seeking out those who have succeeded, or seeing how you might do it differently?

What is your perspective on both your 'want's that you're not doing, and those 'shoulds' that you're living?

How might you change your perspective to see your situation from a different angle, or in a different light?

What are you putting ahead of what you actually want to achieve, because you feel you 'should'?

What is your time and energy spent doing and creating ~ is it your 'shoulds', your 'wants', or distraction and procrastination activities?

Where can you shift the balance a little?

Are you focused on what you don't have, or what you believe? Or are you focused on what you do have, what you can do, and what is true for you?

Is your focus on fixing here and now, or on creating what you envision for your future?

Staying Safe or Future Focus?

The place we are NOW, is often our 'safe space' ... ironically this appears true to your brain even if it is *not* a safe, secure, or healthy, space or situation. Often the unknown appears more scary than a situation that may actually be a threat to us, physically, mentally, or emotionally.

Human beings are incredibly good at adapting to what we have, and becoming comfortable, or 'safe', there, because at least we know what we might expect.

What is it that keeps you in a safe space, even in areas in which you say that you want to make changes? How long have you been saying you want to change your job, or relationship status, or write that book, or whatever it is that you're dissatisfied with but aren't changing?

What excuses are you using for not changing those shoulds into wants, or not taking action on your 'wants' to create them?

"It's just who I am" is one of my favourites ... that's great if you're happy and everything in your life is the way you want it and everything works, but if you're not, and it doesn't, then you're identifying with a thing that doesn't work, that holds you back, with something that creates more of the same and keeps you stuck in your rut.

What's wrong with changing a little bit about the way you approach, or do, things?

You might be thinking "I'm not going to change who I am".

It's not about changing *who* we are ... but about the *way* we look at, express, and go about things, to create a better life for ourselves. This *might* have an effect on how we live, or how others perceive us and therefore it *may* end up seeming like we've changed. However, we're not necessarily re-inventing the wheel here, more like changing the tyres, or even just re-grooving the tread on the tyres, to help us get a better grip.

If we keep doing the same thing, expecting the results to change, we are going to be severely disappointed and keep blaming 'life' and those around us.

If you don't want to change, if you feel "It's just who I am" then it's time to get comfortable with how life is, the more you identify with who you have been up until now, the more you'll stay there.

The more we identify with something that holds us back, the more of that thing we tend to create, so if we think and say things like:

"I'm a hoarder, I like stuff" - throwing stuff away becomes harder, you never know when you might need it, so you hoard more stuff.

"I'm not a talker" – when you want to talk, you feel like you can't – because it's not what people expect from you. More than that, people probably talk over you if you try, because they're not used to hearing you. So, you don't talk.

"I'm just a comfort eater" – each little snack isn't noticed, and more and more things require comfort.

"I am strong and independent" – the more you take on, and/or the more alone you become, the more no-one offers to help because you usually turn them down with an 'I can do it.'

"I'm weird" – the more you ostracise yourself, even if you want to join in the fun, the more 'weird' you become to show you don't care.

"I'm nice" – the more you get frustrated if you want to stand up for yourself or say 'no' – because you don't want to be seen as 'not nice', the 'nicer' you become in the hope that someone will ask you if you're OK, but you're so nice they probably don't.

There are so many ways we label ourselves, or accept labels others put on us. Whatever it is that gives us a label which we are at ease with, or accept, that also gives us an 'out' for not making the change.

"It's who I am".

But it's not always who we are… sometimes who we are, is what we have 'put on' to deal with 'stuff' when it has come up in our life.

Sometimes we 'put on' that attribute so young, we can't remember being any other way; or we have worn it so long we forget we created the identity in response to dealing with a situation in the first place.

What is the fear, belief, or expectation around what will happen if you clear your space? Or become successful? Or earn more money? Or get fitter/lose weight? Or whatever it is that's on your life-should list.

"If I eat more healthily, I won't be able to have fun food ever again"?

"If I stop drinking (or drink less) I'll be boring/lose my social life"?

"If I get rid of my 'stuff' then I'll have to actually do the next thing on my list"?

"If I'm successful I'll have further to fall if it fails"?

"If I lose weight, what if I put it back on again"?

"If I let people know I don't want to do 'x', I'll let them down / they'll hate me / I won't belong"?

"If I write that book, I might have to publish it and if no-one buys it I'll feel rejected and like a failure"?

I don't know … I'm making this up.

I have no idea what it is that's stopping you – but as much as some of our shoulds and life-shoulds belong to other people, so do some of our fears, beliefs and expectations, even if that 'other' person is a younger version of ourselves that no longer serves us.

Should, Want & Your Confident Voice

A lot of the things that no longer serve us are also connected to how we express ourselves, both personally and professionally.

Now that you've got more clarity on what you want, I ask you, where have you been blocked around expressing that in the past? Maybe choose one of your wants and look at who you need to talk to, to make that happen. What might get in the way of talking to them? How confident are you in asking for what you need?

The core of the work I do is around finding out a) what it is you want to say and b) what blocks you from saying it. It is only after that has been discovered that we work on the technical elements of speaking. What you want to say is not just the words, but the effect or result you want them to have; this is important as this shapes the tone of the conversation, and where it comes from in both your body & mind.

When you know what the blocks are, you see your situation from a different perspective. This enables you to adapt the way you respond to the situations you are in, or people you need to address, in order to create what you want.

Now that you've got tools to help you listen to your inner voice, how do you go about expressing it? If some of your wants are around being heard more, or if you need to speak to others in order to start taking action on creating what you want, then finding the right way to express yourself, coming from a place of confidence, clarity and with the conviction of your inner truth, is vital.

Many of the fears and beliefs around what will happen if you say what you want, ask for what you need, express how you feel, or if you share an idea or an opinion, are based in how you were received when you expressed yourself in childhood.

Working with my vocal confidence clients over the past few years has shown me several patterns, but the most interesting are:

Pattern 1

Most people who have a fear of public speaking have something that happened, usually at school and usually between the ages of 7 and 12, which is the key to why they now hate, or get nervous before, speaking in front of an audience. It doesn't have to be something traumatic, or even very big, but it is there in the back of your brain and your body often remembers it as something that requires you to prepare for 'fight or flight'.

Remember, an audience can be as few as one or two people, it doesn't have to be standing up in front of people either, it can be as simple as sitting around a table in a small work meeting and sharing information. One client's trigger was that she had a teacher staring at her while she was reading something out over the school Tannoy system one day. This led to her hating being looked at when speaking, not knowing what others were thinking of her and getting really nervous about it – to the extent of taking beta-blockers before team meetings! (Needless to say, she neither remembered this event as the trigger until we worked on where her fears came from, nor takes beta-blockers any more!)

Pattern 2

If the challenge is less with 'public' speaking, but more around communication, or expressing yourself either to your team, friends, or family, those situations also tend to go back to our youth, but are more around your role in family, or close friendship groups. This is often connected to your life-beliefs and what you needed to do, or not do, in order to 'fit in', or be accepted.

For example, a client who runs their own business didn't express their frustration with people, or situations, because they had a belief that if you express anger in any way, then, you will not be loved. The effect of this repression led to several challenging elements in both their personal and professional life, but included resentment building up, situations not being dealt with, and in some cases family rifts and firing of staff.

Pattern 3

The final challenge is about appearing TOO confident, possibly a bit 'bullish', aloof, or arrogant. This is often about either being defensive (putting up barriers so people can't hurt you, or don't see the 'real' you) or, being so focused on what *you* want and how you think things 'should' be done, that you forget others might have something beneficial to contribute.

I have had a couple of clients like this, male and female, who 'didn't see the point' of small-talk, or asking others when they clearly already knew the answer. Stuck in their 'shoulds', these clients didn't see that sometimes, there might be easier ways to achieve what they 'want'.

There are other elements that effect communication and vocal confidence, but these three patterns are the main ones I see.

One person may have a combination of each of these, depending on the situation you are in, you will be affected differently with how you express what you want. In some situations you will be supremely confident, and in others, you will feel like the new kid in school, where everyone knows everything and you don't know how things work. This is normal, because some things you do every day, some things you know and deal with all the time, and others are new and we all get uncertain and/or nervous in situations that are new, or challenging.

Which one of these patterns resonates most closely for you and any challenges you have with expressing yourself or creating what you want? Whichever of these sounds, or feels, most familiar to you is probably your default position. It is not that it is 'bad', it is just a response to past experiences.

Each of the above is your brain's way of trying to protect you from something that has either been a challenge in the past, or which it perceives may be a threat to you fitting in with the 'tribe'. If you are actively going to start creating your desires, then these are responses that will no longer serve you, so it's time to take a breath, focus on the end result you want to create, and start exploring with speaking your truth and expressing what you need.

Moving Forward

So what next?

Hopefully reaching this point in the book, you've completed the exercises and recognised and reduced how many 'shoulds' you have in your life.

Hopefully you have changed some of the other 'shoulds' in to 'wants' and started to think about how to transform that 'want' in to a reality, how to create that thing in your life.

Hey – even if that thing is doing the laundry, these things are in our life, and changing the way you look at them can change your state: getting on top of your laundry (or delegating it to someone else) might create time in your life for something you want to do more.

Your wanting to do things, with the lighter energy that brings, rather than doing them out of 'duty', may even change the state of others around you. If you feel the success of achieving your wants, how will that change how you are perceived as a person to be around?

If you are working towards your desires, rather than always begrudging the tasks you feel like you 'have' to do, who might you inspire?

If you ask someone for help with something and they feel empowered by that, what effect might that have for all?

If you speak up in a team meeting and spark a debate that solves a problem, might you start getting that recognition you're looking for?

Hopefully by now you're also open to the concept that we can give ourselves more chances to enjoy what we do; even those things that are a duty and we sometimes feel obliged by. It is possible to create a list of options that help you increase the likelihood of *wanting* and then taking action on that want.

You can also keep re-making those choices until you find what works for you.

Or, and here's an important point, **you *can* choose to change nothing in your life** and accept *that* is a choice too; to stay with whatever you have for now, even if it feels like a heavy 'should'.

If you don't change things, then things will stay the same until the universe sends that wake-up call and someone, or something, in life changes things for you.

If you don't listen to your inner voice and express yourself, or take that opportunity to deliver a presentation, tell people what you do and what you're good at, stand up to someone who has put you down, let someone know what's really going on underneath, express yourself clearly; then people won't know what you're thinking, feeling, or capable of, and can't change their perspective of you.

We can't control everything that comes along in our life, but we can take control of how we look at those things and *respond* to them, rather than react.

We all have different lives, different ways of living and different levels of care, or need, for different things to be in our lives.

We all have different levels of what we're prepared to do and not do, to change or not change, to say, or not say, in order to create and live the life we want.

We all have different levels of where we already are in our lives, with different outlooks, natures, cultures and responsibilities.

There is no right or wrong way to live, it's just more or less 'right', rewarding, fulfilling, enjoyable; or 'wrong', frustrating, depressing, destructive, for *you.*

Not changing things is a choice too.

And that's OK by me, if it's OK with you.

Which door do you choose?

A by no means exhaustive list of common 'shoulds' (from my survey):

I SHOULD:

Lose weight

Exercise more / Get fit / Go to the gym

Eat more healthily / Eat less junk

Stop smoking

Drink less

Be married by now

Have children

Have a better job

Earn more

Have my own home

Get up earlier

Go to bed earlier

Save more money

Buy less 'stuff'

Get a social life

Learn a language

Be 'x' by now

Be in a relationship

Take up a hobby

Spend more time with 'x'

Visit 'y'

Stay in touch with friends and family better

Be better / more successful in my business

Be doing more of everything!! (Seriously a few people said this)

Have more 'me' time ... (so do less of everything??)

Be better at 'x'

Be a better partner / parent

Believe in myself

Clean the house / car

Create more time / Manage time better

Do my admin

Not compare myself to others so much

Judge people less

Stop procrastinating

Work harder

Play more

Write 'x, y or z'

Stop being so hard on myself ….

What do you WANT to do????

Love and blessings

JQ x

Message from the Author

"Hello!"

This is my first book and I hope you have found it useful, enlightening, or at the very least, that it has helped you look at things in your life in a slightly different light.

I created "Stop Shoulding. Start Wanting" as an introduction to a few mindset and coaching tools which are easy to implement, to help you connect to your inner voice and start creating the change you want to see in your life.

It's great to know what it is you want, and it is the first step to finding your voice and making a difference in your life. However, to 'want' does mean to not have, so you need to make choices to change that want in to 'create'. It's likely there'll be another book along at some point about that, but if you don't want to wait for that…

If you like my style and want to delve deeper in to making choices, or discovering and liberating your confident voice, I offer coaching programmes that support this work. (Other coaches are available!)

Working with a coach means having someone in your life who is there, without judgment, to support and keep you accountable, to help you own your choices and move away from 'Duty' towards your desires.

If you would like to explore those programmes or my workshops, if you want support with creating or delivering a speech or presentation, or to experience my sound healing, sonic meditation, or tailor-made VIP days, then get in touch. I would love to support you to reconnect to the power of being in your whole self and to discover your whole, confident, voice, whether that's discovering what you want in life, speaking in public, or expressing yourself to others.

In the meantime, it really helps to stop 'should-ing', so without further ado I'll let you get on with it and look forward to hearing from you.

Best & Blessings

Judith x

To find out more about me, the work I do, and some free voice-tools to download visit my website www.YourWholeVoice.com where you can also sign up to my monthly missive newsletter and keep up to date with what I'm doing, get news and special offers

Follow me on Facebook here

www.facebook.com/YourWholevoice

About the Illustrator:

Erica Webb is a Melbourne, Australia-based illustrator who draws on her curiosity for the world and the people inhabiting it to fuel her love of drawing and creating.

Through her pictures, she hopes to encourage children and adults alike to look with wonder and appreciation at their world and the people they share it with. She is also the mother of two young boys and a yoga teacher. ~

You can find more of Erica's work and connect with her at www.ericawebb.com.au

Acknowledgments:

It's not the Olivier's, or the Oscars, but I have a few thank-yous to those without whom this book would not have been possible. It's my first book – the list is too long – I've probably still forgotten people – apologies in advance!

My mum – who has read this book and knows about the things I put in here; she's bloody brilliant. She never even once told me I shouldn't be an actress, just maybe concerned about how I would survive... (mind you, I think she still worries about my job security and I'm still working on a few of my 'shoulds' that I've inherited around that!)

Dad – I've always said I wouldn't be who I am, if you hadn't been who you are ... it's not always been easy, it's been a journey – but look where we got to.

J, Paul, Kev & Av – the best siblings I have. LOVE YOU ALL xxx

(Extra props to you Paul for getting me out of a tight spot ... See, the book got printed ... who knows, you may yet get a return on your investment)!

Jen Brister, comic and friend extraordinaire, for your unending faith in me, for being my champion and listening to all my ideas. "This is going to be our year!"

Erica, my fabulous illustrator, you put my faith in the best parts of the internet and the fact that

I'm in the right FB groups – glad I found you, you rocked it.

To Sarah Bolas of Potential Consulting, amazing woman, great friend, and the person who told me I was already coaching when I didn't know what coaching was – see what you created!

To all the friends who know all the parts of me and still love me anyway – sorry for my crazy diary and unavailability (since always, I know) and to the friend who triggered my 'blip' in the summer of 2016 … I took myself to the darkest places and I brought myself back out again – I didn't know I needed to go there, thank you.

HUGE thanks to those of you who read draft 3, did the exercises, and gave me honest feedback so I knew if I even had something that people might find useful. I hope you like the changes … your free copy of the finished article is on its way!

Without my coaching training at The Coaching Academy I wouldn't have realised that other people 'don't should' too, or started doing this work with the confidence that a recognised qualification gave me.

For the training of William Whitecloud and Ryan Pinnick of Natural Success/Supergenius. Implementing your work has helped me create structure for myself, make my first corporate client, got me out of my acute depressive 'blip' in summer 2016, which lead to a deeper healing my relationship with my dad.

What's obvious? End Results right here! Thanks to ALL my Genius friends for your support - Hold the tension.

Sammy Blindell of How To Build a Brand, without the massive kick in to action I got when I won that competition in your FB group at the start of 2017, I'm not sure I'd have the business, the clarity and direction that I have found, let alone got around to actually find a publisher for this book! The amazing support network and friends I have found in the brilliant bunch of people that make up the Brand Builders Club – thank you for the safe space to share ideas and make mistakes. "BOOM!"

Thank you to Marie Diamond, for your kind words in the forward, for seeing something in me that I didn't see in myself – that I am a transformational leader – I was honoured to accept your invitation to join the Association of Transformational Leaders of Europe and delight in the friendship and support I have found there.

To everyone who has supported me through this intense year of 2017, which has been massive: for the international speaking gigs, online summits, interviews and workshops, guest-speaker slots, award nominations & wins, for the ears that listened when I was overwhelmed, the walks in the park, the treating to dinner when I was skint, for the chilling out time and Kali-cat-sitting, for all of it and so much more – I thank you.

To anyone who ever bullied me, tried to belittle me, put me down, suggested I wasn't good enough, turned me down, pushed me away, questioned my choices, or otherwise created challenges in my life that added to my belief systems ... I wouldn't be who I am today without every experience I've had in my life – so you played your part and I'm grateful.

Just two more thanks to come:

Firstly, to Sean Patrick of That Guy's House – from a random email I sent to you having seen a FB post from another of your authors, to becoming the fabulous, supportive, hugely enthusiastic publisher of this book – THANK YOU!

Finally, of course, to YOU, the reader.

Without you this is a futile exercise. There are a lot of people out there writing books 'to have a book, not a business card' ~ I say a big swear word beginning with B and sounding like 'sollocks' to that.

I wrote this book FOR YOU – to help you get some of the clarity I discovered when I started coaching, to acknowledge and establish awareness of the barriers in your life and beliefs, to see what it is that you really want, and to start listening to your own voice ...

So, thank YOU for taking the time to put yourself in the centre of your life and for each step you take towards knowing, creating and expressing your wants.

Are you ready to stop 'shoulding' and start wanting?

Are you ready to start taking action on those wants and get creating?

Have you started to find your voice?

Are you ready to use it?

GREAT!

See you soon x

Lightning Source UK Ltd.
Milton Keynes UK
UKHW020750060521
383241UK00016B/1574